FLORAL
CROSS STITCH

FLORAL
CROSS STITCH

MELINDA COSS

ANAYA PUBLISHERS LTD
LONDON

*To the folks of Gwernogle (Place of Alders),
where, because of their gentleness,
'even the most troubled spirit can find rest'.*
LLANFIHANGEL LEGENDS, *REV. PATRICK THOMAS (1989)*

First published in Great Britain in 1993 by
Anaya Publishers Limited, Strode House
44–45 Osnaburgh Street, London NW1 3ND

British Library Cataloguing in Publication Data
Coss, Melinda   *Floral Cross Stitch*
I. Title   746.44

ISBN 1-85470-013-8

Designed by Studio Gossett
Cover design by Carole Perks
Edited by Lydia Darbyshire
Photography by Di Lewis
Co-ordination and styling by Di Lewis
Charts drawn by John Hutchinson
Plant illustrations by Rosanne Sanders
Technique illustrations by John Hutchinson
Typeset in Great Britain by Servis Filmsetting Ltd, Manchester
Colour reproduction by Scantrans Pte. Ltd., Singapore

Printed and bound in China

CONTENTS

INTRODUCTION

Pinned to the wall of my studio is a 6-inch (15cm) square, orange Aida needlecase. It is decorated with a multicoloured border in cross stitch, and the word MUM is embroidered in the centre in bright red. I also have a cross stitch cushion in blue and yet another in cream. It's impossible for me to remember now if these were produced by me for my mother or by my children for me. The interesting thing is that, through two generations, these humble offerings of patience and creativity have survived.

I often ask myself how I ended up making a career from needlecrafts. At school I absolutely hated them. I can remember when I was aged five or six, while the boys were enjoying themselves banging nails into bits of wood, the girls had to sit on the floor in a circle and count holes in pieces of canvas, victims to teacher's harsh recriminations if knots should be discovered in the back of the work. If I suffered in the 1950s, how, I wonder, did Victorian children cope with the hours and hours of discipline required to produce their wonderful samplers? And why is it that such a painful childhood experience can re-emerge in adulthood as a pleasurable pastime, indeed, as an activity to which one looks forward at the end of a busy day?

The answers are to be found in the samplers, in my colourful bits of cross stitch and in any piece of craft work that survives for generations and through changing values. The most important fact is that, more often than not, they do survive and, in surviving, provide us, the makers, or the recipients with enduring images of our achievements and memories of the investment in time, care and patience that were put into them. Add the pleasure and satisfaction gained from self-expression, and it becomes understandable why many stitchers are obsessive about their work. In my own case, the pleasure also comes from the triumph of industry over inherent idleness. If even *I* managed to complete my needlework to teacher's satisfaction, anything was possible.

This book of floral designs is intended to be inspirational. I am not your teacher, and I hope only that, by presenting some of my favourite flowers in particular ways, I can encourage you to use them as a basis for your own designs. Many flowers have significant sentiments attached to them, and you might want to consider these when you are embroidering a gift for a loved one. I've embroidered many a forget-me-not card for belated birthdays and even a snapdragon apology for someone I was rude to!

First, you should decide what you wish to make. You may want to embroider your bed linen or make a framed picture. Don't be limited by my use of single motifs – the fuchsia, for example, could be repeated horizontally to form a border, or you could take the honeysuckle spray from the panelled table-cloth and use it on a greetings card. I'm particularly pleased with the primula cross stitch sewing tidy, and, of course, you could use any of the motifs in this book to make a tidy of your own design. 'Have tidy, will travel' – and the beauty of cross stitch is that it is portable. There need be no more wasted hours sitting on trains or in dentists' waiting rooms, and in the summer you can lounge on your deckchair, getting a tan and stitching greetings cards at the same time.

Second, you should think about the basic fabric you are going to use, as this will have a huge influence on your finished work. Enchanted by the linens embroidered in the 1930s and 1940s, I was inclined to produce all these designs on Irish linen or fine cotton. Using waste canvas makes it possible to work in cross stitch on virtually any fabric. However, Aida and special evenweave fabrics are widely available and a delight to work on, so I have used a variety of materials to give you some idea of the different effects that can be achieved. Pure linen is expensive to buy, so look out for it at flea markets, jumble sales and auctions, where you might pay pennies instead of pounds or dollars. Lace and ribbons can greatly enhance your finished work and should be treasured when they are discovered attached to garments that are about to be discarded.

As with my book *Floral Needlepoint*, I have had a fascinating time researching the origins of the flowers and their folklore. I hope you will enjoy reading my discoveries and that I have included some of your favourites.

Happy stitching!

Melinda Coss

ANEMONE JAR TOP

Despite its associations with unhappiness, the anemone remains one of my personal favourites, not least because of its wonderful colours. This small design can be used as a corner motif or centre-piece on many items.

The poppy-flowered anemone, *Anemone coronaria*, is also sometimes known as the windflower. Greek legends say that Anemos, the wind, sends his namesakes, the anemones, in the earliest spring days as an emblem of his coming, while in Greek mythology the wood anemone, *Anemone nemorosa*, is said to have sprung from the tears of Venus as she wandered through the woodlands, weeping for the death of Adonis. Anemone was also the name of a nymph beloved by Zephyr, the west wind, who aroused the jealousy of Flora. Anemone was banished from Flora's court and changed into a flower, which always blossoms before the return of spring. Zephyr abandoned her to the rough caress of Boreas, the north wind. Boreas failed to win Anemone's love but disturbed her emotions, so now she blooms too early and fades too quickly.

Anemone pulsatilla (*Pulsatilla vulgaris*) is also known as the Easter flower or the pasque flower because it appears around this time. The juice of the purple sepals of this rare plant produces a green dye that was used to stain paper and linen, but the colour is not permanent. The dye was also used to colour Easter eggs in some European countries.

The ancient Egyptians regarded the wood anemone as the emblem of sickness, perhaps from the flush of colour upon the backs of the white sepals, and the Chinese call it the 'Flower of Death'. In some European countries it was looked on by peasants as a flower of ill-omen, although the reasons for the superstition are obscure.

Culpeper, quoting Gerard, offered the following use for this unhappy flower:

> The body being bathed with the decoction of the leaves cures the leprosy: the leaves being stamped and the juice snuffed up the nose purgeth the head mightily; so doth the root, being chewed in the mouth, for it procureth much spitting and bringeth away many watery and phlegmatic humours, and is therefore excellent for the lethargy. . . . Being made into an ointment and the eyelids anointed with it, it helps inflammation of the eyes. The same ointment is excellent good to cleanse malignant and corroded ulcers. . . . And when all is done, let physicians prate what they please, all the pills in the dispensary purge not the head like to hot things held in the mouth.

The anemone is, however, a member of the buttercup family and, like other members of that family, is poisonous to animals and humans. The juice can cause an allergic reaction on the skin of sensitive people.

In the language of flowers anemone means 'forsaken'.

COMMON NAMES: windflower; *Anemone nemorosa*: crowfoot, smell fox; *Anemone pulsatilla*: pasque flower, meadow anemone, passe flower, Easter flower.

Coy Anemone, that ne're uncloses,
Her lips until they're blown on
by the wind.
ANON

MATERIALS

1 piece of 28-count tea-coloured linen,
    4 × 4in (10 × 10cm)
Framecraft cut glass jar with 3in (7.5cm)
    diameter lid (see Stockist Information)
Anchor stranded cotton – use 2 strands
    throughout

- 20in (50cm) black (403)
- 20in (50cm) blue-green (205)
- 20in (50cm) green (230)
- 20in (50cm) mauve (89)
- 20in (50cm) pale green (206)
- 20in (50cm) crimson (13)
- 20in (50cm) blue (131)
- 20in (50cm) red (333)
- 20in (50cm) violet (111)

DESIGN SIZE
2¾ × 2¾in (7 × 7cm)

METHOD

Fold the linen in half, then in half again to find the centre. Mark the centre of the chart and work outwards from this point. Stitch using two strands of cotton and working crosses over two strands of linen, both vertically and horizontally. Follow the chart in cross stitch throughout.

MAKING UP

Cut the linen to fit the size of the jar and fix it in place according to the manufacturer's instructions.

ANTIRRHINUM STATIONERY HOLDER

This colourful bunch of snapdragons can be used as a folder for stationery or as a cover for a sketch book. The design would look equally attractive as a framed picture or as the centre-piece of a cushion.

A welcome summer flower, *Antirrhinum majus* is popularly known as snapdragon because the flower's opening is like a dragon's mouth. It is also sometimes called calf's snout, since its head resembles the nose and mouth of a calf. The generic name, too, derives from the flower's resemblance to an animal's mouth, coming from the Greek *anti* (counterfeiting) and *rhinos* (nose).

Together with toadflax, snapdragon was highly valued in olden times as a preservative against witchcraft. According to Thistleton Dyer (*The Folk-Lore of Plants*, 1889), 'the flower possesses the power of destroying charms and causes maledictions uttered against the person using it to fail of their purpose'.

Mrs Grieve notes that the plant has bitter and stimulant properties and that 'the leaves of this and several allied species have been employed on the Continent in cataplasms to tumours and ulcers'.

Snapdragon seeds should be planted in well-drained garden soil in a sunny spot in summer or seedlings should be planted out in autumn. In the language of flowers antirrhinum means 'presumption'.

COMMON NAMES: snapdragon, calf's snout.

Trinity had never been unkind to me. There used to be much snap-dragon growing on the walls opposite my freshman's rooms there, and I had for years taken it as the emblem of my own perpetual residence even unto death in my University.

APOLOGIA PRO VITA SUA *(1864), JOHN HENRY, CARDINAL NEWMAN (1801–90)*

MATERIALS

1 piece of 26-count cream linen,
  18 × 11in (45.5 × 28cm)
2 pieces of cardboard, 8½ × 10in
  (21.5 × 25cm) each
2 pieces of felt or wallpaper, 8½ × 10in
  (21.5 × 25cm) each
1in (2.5cm) wide heavy-duty adhesive
  tape
1yd (1m) pink cord
Rubber-based adhesive
Anchor stranded cotton – use 2 strands
  throughout

DESIGN SIZE
7 × 5½in (17.5 × 13cm)

40in (100cm) green (227)
40in (100cm) dark green (230)
40in (100cm) yellow (298)
40in (100cm) dusty mauve (970)
40in (100cm) cherry (799)
40in (100cm) wine (897)
20in (50cm) light green (205)
20in (50cm) rust (326)
20in (50cm) gold (304)
20in (50cm) tan (884)
20in (50cm) mustard (307)
20in (50cm) rose (894)
20in (50cm) pink (25)
20in (50cm) fuchsia (57)

METHOD

Fold the linen in half and crease the fold. Open up the linen and fold the right-hand section (the front of the folder) in half again and then in half lengthways to find the centre. Mark the centre of the chart and work outwards from this point. Stitch using two strands of cotton and working crosses over two strands of linen both vertically and horizontally. Follow the chart in cross stitch throughout.

MAKING UP

Place the two sheets of cardboard side by side and use adhesive tape to join them at the centre to form a folder. Open out the piece of linen with the wrong side of the cross stitch facing you and put the joined sheets of cardboard on top. Lay the cord down the centre join, leaving equal lengths of loose cord at the top and bottom. Fold over and glue the raw edges of the linen to the card. Cut four strips, each measuring approximately 8½ × 1in (21.5 × 2.5cm), from the pieces of felt or wallpaper, making oblongs to cover the inside of the cover. Place the strips diagonally across the top and bottom corners of the oblongs of wallpaper or felt, folding back the ends and sticking them to the back of the main pieces. Glue the lining to the inside of the folder to cover all raw edges and folds of linen. Tie the cord back to the right side and fasten it in a bow.

Too quick despairer, wherefore wilt thou go?
Soon will the high Midsummer pomps come on,
Soon will the musk carnations break and smell,
Soon shall we have gold-dusted snapdragon,
Sweet-William with his homely cottage-smell,
And stocks in fragrant blow.
THYRSIS,
MATTHEW ARNOLD (1822–88)

BASKET OF ROSES AND FORGET-ME-NOTS

This small design is perfect for keepsakes, whether they are greetings cards, pin cushions or brooches. Adjust the count of the canvas you use to get the most mileage from this pretty basket of flowers.

ROSE

Medieval legend asserts that the first roses appeared miraculously at Bethlehem as a result of the prayers of a 'fayre Mayden' who had been accused and sentenced to death by burning. After her prayers, Sir John Mandeville relates, 'sche entered into the Fuyer . . . and the Brondes that weren brennynge, becomen red Roseres; and the Brondes that weren not kyndled, becomen white Roseres. . . . And thus was the Mayden saved.'

A rosebud of any kind suggests hope, promise and youthful beauty, while roses generally signify beauty, bliss, elegance, flame, fragrance, frailty, joy,

life, pleasure, pomp, praise, prayer, pride, secrecy, silence, a star, the sun, wine, wisdom and woman.

Particular roses are birthday flowers for different dates, and if you are sending roses as a birthday gift, you should take the following into account: a yellow rose is the birthday flower for 2 February; the red rose of Lancaster is for 5 June; a white rosebud is for 6 July and a red rosebud (signifying pure and inclined to love) is for 7 July; the white rose (signifying purity, silence and virginity) is for 8 July; the Burgundy rose (signifying simplicity and beauty) is for 1 August; the hundred-leaf rose, *Rosa centifolia*, is for 5 August; the Damask rose (signifying bashful love) is for 12 August; the red rose is for 13 October; and the China rose (which signifies grace or beauty ever fresh) is for 14 October.

A wreath of roses represents beauty and virtue rewarded, while a dried white rose means death in preference to loss of innocence. A full-blown rose stands for beauty and engagement, and a rose leaf signifies 'you may hope'. A rose thorn means pain and death; it is also a Christian symbol of sin.

FORGET-ME-NOT

A Persian story describes how an angel sat weeping at the Gates of Light, for he had loved a daughter of the earth and so forfeited his place in heaven. He had first seen the girl at the river's edge, decorating her hair with forget-me-nots, and, as a punishment for losing his heart to her, he was barred from paradise until the woman had planted forget-me-nots in every corner of the world. It was a tedious task but, through her great love, she undertook it, and so for years, in all climes and weathers, they wandered over the globe together, planting this little flower. When the task was ended the couple returned to the Gates of Light and, behold, they were not closed against them. The woman was admitted without death, 'For,' said the keepers of the way, 'your love is greater than your wish for life; and as he on whom you have bestowed yourself is an angel, so love of the heavenly has raised you above corruption. Enter into the joys of heaven, the greatest of which is unselfish love.'

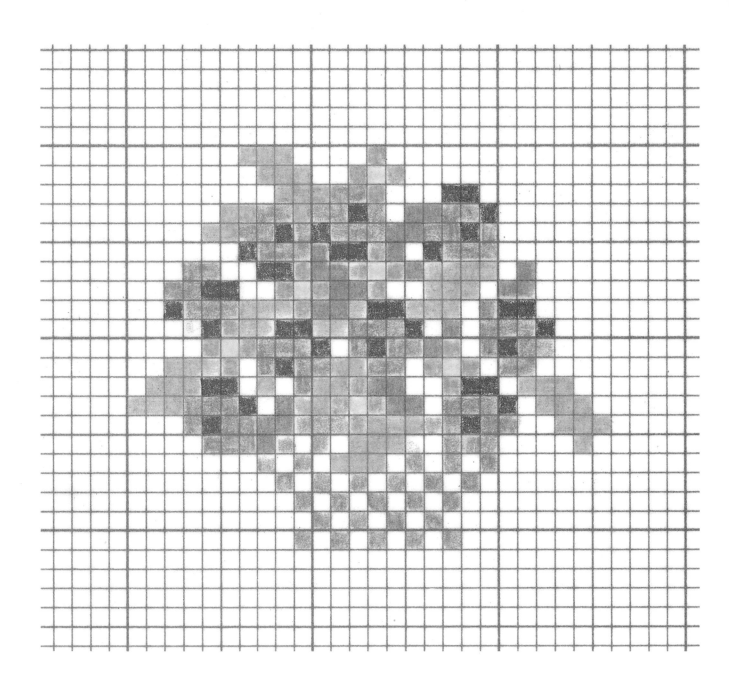

MATERIALS

1 piece of 26-count cream or white linen,
  4 × 4in (10 × 10cm)
1 circular frame, 2in (5cm) in diameter
  or 1 oval brooch mount, 2 × 1½in
  (5 × 3.75cm)
Medium-weight cardboard
Rubber-based adhesive
1 piece of felt, 4 × 4in (10 × 10cm)
Anchor stranded cotton – use 2 strands
  throughout for picture **or** 1 strand
  throughout for brooch, for which only
  half the listed quantities are required

- 20in (50cm) fuchsia (87)
- 20in (50cm) pink (85)
- 20in (50cm) green (255)
- 20in (50cm) blue-green (205)
- 20in (50cm) blue (129)
- 20in (50cm) camel (362)
- 12in (30cm) yellow (289)

DESIGN SIZE
Framed picture – 2 × 1¾in (5 × 4cm);
brooch – 1 × ¾in (2.5 × 2cm)

PICTURE

M·E T H O D

Fold the linen in half and then in half again to find the centre. Mark the centre stitch on the chart and work outwards from this point. Stitch using two strands of cotton and working over two strands of linen both vertically and horizontally. Work in cross stitch throughout.

MAKING UP

Cut the cardboard to fit the inside of the frame and mount the finished design on the cardboard, securing the waste edges at the back with a rubber-based adhesive. Back it with felt to cover the raw edges and fix the design into the frame.

BROOCH

M E T H O D

Work as for the picture, but use only one strand of cotton and work over one strand of linen both vertically and horizontally. Mount as for the picture or following the manufacturer's instructions.

BUTTERCUPS AND DAISIES TABLE-CLOTH

Nothing can be more pleasing than a bunch of freshly picked field flowers, and this delicate bouquet of buttercups, daisies and harebells will brighten any morning. I have used this motif on a breakfast-time table-cloth, but you could work the design on a smaller scale to make a pretty greetings card.

BUTTERCUP

The dazzling yellow flowers of the buttercup, *Ranunculus repens*, are so named because they were once supposed to increase the butter content of milk. In fact, cattle refuse to eat buttercups, which have an unpleasant taste and are probably poisonous to them. Nevertheless, it is a long-standing tradition that if you hold a buttercup under your chin, the gold reflection will show whether or not you like butter.

Like other members of its family, the buttercup can inflame and irritate the skin, and it was this property that caused it to be applied to gouty joints. In the Middle Ages the roots were ground with salt as a cure for the plague – the mixture caused blisters, which were thought to draw out the disease – while a bag filled with buttercups and hung around the neck was said to cure lunacy.

The buttercup is the flower of cheerfulness, childishness and ingratitude, and in the language of flowers buttercup means 'childhood'.

COMMON NAMES: St Anthony's turnip, crowfoot, frogsfoot, goldcup.

Like the buttercup, the daisy, *Bellis perennis*, is said to be a flower of children, and in Scotland it is known as bairnwort. The small double daisy that grows in such profusion in our gardens was said by Wordsworth to be the 'poet's darling'.

In the language of flowers daisy means 'I share your sentiments, I reciprocate your affections', and this symbolism goes back to the days of knightly tournaments, when the daisy was considered to be a valued emblem. When a lady granted a knight permission to emblazon a double daisy on his shield it was a public statement that she returned his affection. A wreath of wild daisies, on the other hand, was worn on the brow of a lady who was considering whether to accept her lover's suit.

The daisy was a great favourite of Geoffrey Chaucer's:

Well by reason men it call maie
The Daisie, or else the eye of the
Daie.
That of alle the floures in the mede,
Than love I most these floures whyte
and rede,
Swiche as men callen daysies in our
toun.

Summer is said to have come when you can put your foot on seven daisies at once, and children have for long made necklaces and garlands of daisies. We must all be familiar with the tradition of plucking petals from a daisy to discover if 'he loves me, he loves me not'. Did you know, though, that most daisies have an odd number of petals, so if you begin with 'he loves me' all will end well? This custom resulted in another of the daisy's common names – measure of love.

This little plant has some less pleasant connotations. It has been seen as the emblem of deceit. In *A Quip for an Upstart Courtier* (1592) Robert Greene spoke of the 'dissembling daisy', and in *Hamlet* Ophelia gives Gertrude a daisy to signify that 'her light and fickle love ought not to expect constancy in her husband'.

Daisies are also believed to ease the wounds of soldiers on the battlefield. 'To lie beneath the daisies' is a metaphor for death, and shortly before he died, the poet John Keats wrote that he felt the daisies growing over him. 'Pushing up the daisies' is another expression for death.

The Celtic physicians of Myddfai believed that you could predict death with the daisy. 'Take the flower of the daisy, and pound well with wine, giving it the patient to drink. If he vomit, he will die of that disease, if not, he will live, and this has proven true.'

COMMON NAMES: bruisewort, bairnwort (Scotland), llygad y dydd (eye of the day, Wales), herb Margaret.

The decoction of the field Daisie (which is the best for physicks use) made in water and drunke, is good against agues.

JOHN GERARD

Another well known prescription for relieving head pains resulting from a fall, a blow or concussion of the brain consists of macerating two handfuls of fresh plant (leaves and flowers) in a litre of white wine for twenty-four hours and drinking a glassful each morning. This treatment is also prescribed for dropsy, rheumatic pains, contusions, sprains, ecchymosis.

JEAN PALAISEUL

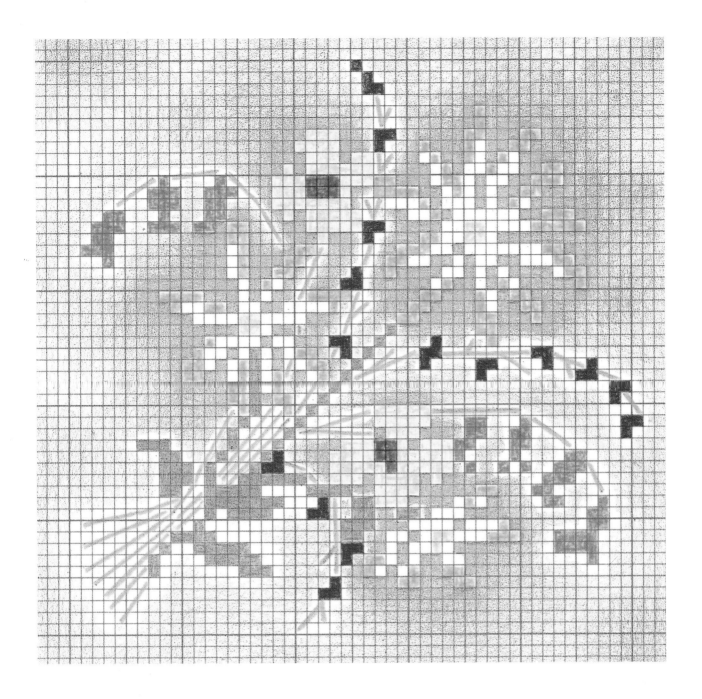

DESIGN SIZE
5½ × 5½in (14 × 14cm)

M A T E R I A L S

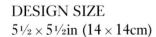

1 cotton table-cloth – the one illustrated
   measures 33 × 33in (84 × 84cm)
4 pieces of 10-hole waste canvas, 6 × 6in
   (15 × 15cm) each
Anchor stranded cotton – use 2 strands
   throughout

☐ 13ft (4m) white (1)

▨ 13ft (4m) pink (24)

▦ 10ft (3m) yellow (298)

▩ 8ft 6in (2.5m) green (255)

▨ 6ft 6in (2m) light green (254)

▨ 6ft 6in (2m) mauve (90)

■ 5ft (1.5m) lavender (109)

▨ 20in (50cm) orange (925)

M E T H O D

Position and tack (baste) one square of waste canvas to each corner of the cloth. Follow the chart in cross stitch, using two strands of cotton and working over two strands of canvas both horizontally and vertically. Work the flower stems in backstitch, using two strands of cotton.

Dampen the completed work and carefully remove the waste canvas. Press lightly over a damp cloth.

Be kind to those dear little folks
When our toes are turned up to the daisies!
THE INGOLDSBY LEGENDS. THE BABES IN THE
WOOD, *REV. RICHARD HARRIS BARHAM (1788–1845)*

All will be gay when noontide wakes anew
The buttercups, the little children's dower
– Far brighter than this gaudy melon-flower!
HOME-THOUGHTS, FROM ABROAD,
ROBERT BROWNING (1812–89)

Buttercups and daisies,
Oh, the pretty flowers;
Coming ere the Springtime,
To tell of sunny hours.
BUTTERCUPS AND DAISIES,
MARY HOWITT (1799–1888)

COLUMBINE
TABLE-CLOTH

This spray of columbines, in their soft colours, can be used as a corner-piece on a table-cloth or runner. You can alter the positions of the flowers to fit any piece of table linen. The photograph shows the motif worked on a table-cloth with a diameter of 67in (170cm) and repeated four times.

The columbine, *Aquilegia vulgaris*, is a favourite old-fashioned garden flower, being mentioned by Thomas Tusser (?1524–80) among a list of flowers suitable 'for windows and pots'; and in 1629 John Parkinson wrote of the many varieties grown in gardens. It was one of the badges of the House of Lancaster and also of the family of Derby.

The generic name, *Aquilegia*, is derived from the Latin *aquila* (an eagle), the spurs of the flowers being considered to resemble an eagle's talons. The popular name, columbine, is from the Latin *columba* (a dove or pigeon), from the idea that the flowers resemble a flight of these birds. A still older name, culverwort, has the same reference, *wort* being the Saxon word for a plant and *culfre* meaning a pigeon.

Culpeper suggested that the leaves of columbine could be successfully used in lotions for sore mouths and throats, and he wrote: 'The Spaniards used to eat a piece of the root thereof in a morning fasting many days together, to help them when troubled with stone. The seed taken in wine with a little saffron removes obstructions of the liver and is good for the yellow jaundice.'

An association has been formed to make this the national flower of the United States, since its common name suggests Columbus and Columbia, while its generic name has associations with the bird of freedom. In addition, the plant can be raised from seed in almost any American garden, and it is native to nearly all the States.

In the language of flowers columbine means 'folly'.

COMMON NAME: culverwort.

Bring cornflag, tulip and Adonis flower,
Fair Oxeye, goldylocks and columbine.
BEN JONSON (1573–1637)

Bring hither the Pink and purple Columbine,
With Gillyflowers:
Bring Coronation, and Sops in wine,
Worn of paramours.
Strew me the ground with Daffadowndillies,
And Cowslips, and Kingcups, and loved Lilies:
The pretty Pawnce,
And the Chevisaunce,
Shall match with the fair flower Delice.
THE SHEPHERD'S CALENDAR, APRIL,
EDMUND SPENSER (?1552–99)

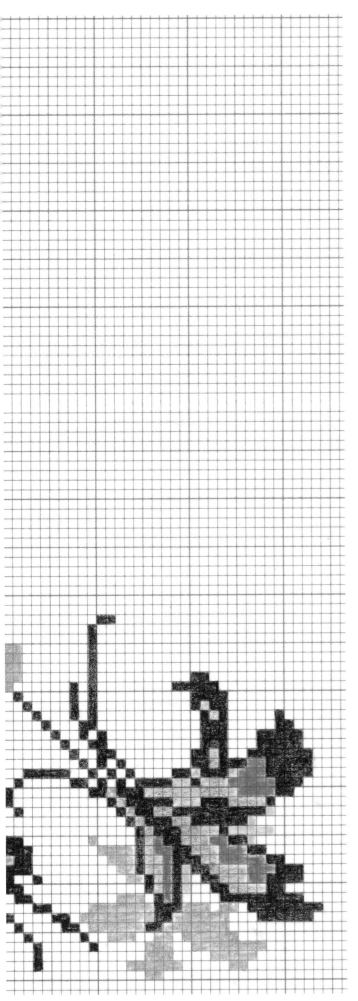

MATERIALS

1 cotton table-cloth – the one illustrated
   is 67in (170cm) in diameter
1 piece of 26-count waste canvas,
   10 × 9in (25 × 23cm), for each motif
Anchor stranded cotton (for each motif)
   – use 2 strands throughout

    10ft (3m) blue (131)

    10ft (3m) fuchsia (57)

    10ft (3m) lilac (107)

    5ft (1.5m) green (255)

    3ft 3in (1m) yellow (305)

    3ft 3in (1m) coral (10)

    3ft 3in (1m) lavender (109)

    30in (75cm) light blue (129)

    30in (75cm) cream (852)

    30in (75cm) pink (85)

DESIGN SIZE
8 × 7½in (20 × 19cm) approximately

METHOD

Tack (baste) the waste canvas to the cloth
in the positions required for your motifs.
Run a thread horizontally and vertically
across each square of canvas waste to
establish the centre, mark the centre of
the chart and work outwards from this
point. Work crosses in two strands of
cotton over two threads of waste canvas
both horizontally and vertically. When the
design is completed, dampen the fabric
and carefully pull out the waste from
under the stitches.

COTTAGE GARDEN NEEDLECASE

This pretty cottage garden contains lupins, geraniums, violets, forget-me-nots and snapdragons. The motif could be used on a book cover, pot pourri sachet or a greetings card, but I've chosen to use it on a simple needlecase.

LUPIN

The lupin (*Lupinus* varieties) has traditionally brightened many an English cottage garden. Such was its popularity, in fact, that in 1917 a 'lupin' banquet was given at a botanical gathering in Hamburg. A German professor, Dr Thoms, described the multifarious uses to which the lupin might be put.

> At a table coverd with a tablecloth of Lupin fibre, Lupin soup was served; after the soup came Lupin beefsteak, roasted in Lupin oil and seasoned with Lupin extract, then bread containing 20 per cent of Lupin, Lupin margarine and cheese of Lupin albumen, and finally Lupin liqueur and Lupin coffee. Lupin soap served for washing the hands, while Lupin-fibre paper and envelopes with Lupin adhesive were available for writing.

According to Dr Fernie's *Herbal Simples* (1897), the seeds were used as a species of money by Roman actors in their plays and comedies, whence came the saying 'nummus lupinus' – a spurious bit of money.

John Parkinson attributed wonderful virtues to the plant: 'Many women doe use the meale of Lupines mingled with the gall of a goate and some juyce of Lemons to make into a forme of a soft ointment. . . . the burning of Lupin seeds drives away gnats.'

COMMON NAME: Wolfsbohne (Germany).

The word violet is a diminutive of *viola*, the Latin form of the Greek name *Ione*. Legend has it that Jupiter changed his beloved Io into a white heifer for fear of Juno's jealousy and caused these modest flowers to spring forth from the earth to be fitting food for her, giving them her name. Another derivation is said to be from the Latin *vias* (wayside). A Greek legend recounts how the violet first sprang up when Orpheus laid down his lute on a mossy bank.

In the past violets were used in a number of ways. They were often included in love charms and philtres; they were candied and eaten as sweetmeats; and they were put into salads and made into syrups, preserves and cordials. Decoctions of the leaves or flowers were used to cure agues, fevers, jaundice, pleurisy and colds. Plasters of the leaves allayed pain, reduced swellings and ulcers, and healed sore throats. *The Book of the Physicians of Myddfai* states that a sure way to discover if an injured man will recover is to bind a bruised violet to his forefinger and watch to see whether he sleeps. If he does, he will live; if not, he will die.

To dream of violets is fortunate, for they foretell a change for the better in the dreamer's circumstances.

In the language of flowers the white violet is emblematic of modesty and innocence, and the blue violet of faithful love. The colour violet indicates the love of truth and the truth of love.

We can use every part of this plant which is so unobtrusive that it has long been the very emblem of modesty.

JEAN PALAISEUL

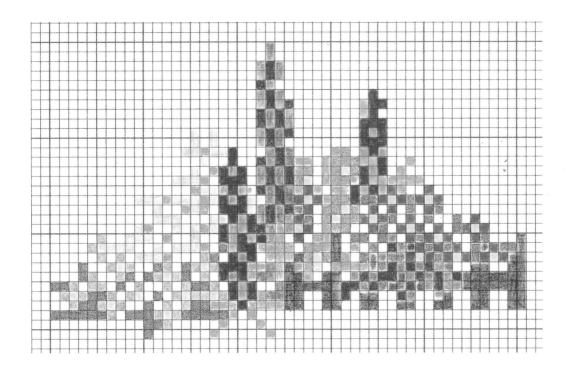

MATERIALS

1 piece of 26-count cream linen,
  6½ × 5in (16.5 × 12.5cm)
Rubber-based adhesive
4 pieces of light coloured felt, 5½ × 4in
  (14 × 10cm) each
20in (50cm) narrow lilac ribbon
Anchor stranded cotton – use 2 strands
  throughout

	30in (75cm) light blue (129)
	30in (75cm) yellow (298)
	20in (50cm) lilac (108)
	20in (50cm) mauve (87)
	20in (50cm) red (335)
	20in (50cm) green (229)
	20in (50cm) blue-green (205)
	20in (50cm) pink (85)
	20in (50cm) purple (110)
	20in (50cm) brown (358)
	10in (25cm) blue (131)

DESIGN SIZE
2½ × 4in (6.5 × 10cm)

METHOD

Fold the linen in half and then in half
again to find the centre. Mark the centre
stitch on the chart and work outwards
from this point. Stitch, using two strands
of cotton and working over two strands of
linen vertically and horizontally. Follow
the chart in cross stitch throughout.

MAKING UP

Fold back ½in (1cm) of linen along all
the edges and catch (baste) into position.
Use a rubber-based adhesive to stick one
of the pieces of felt to the back of the
finished needlepoint. Lay the other three
pieces of felt on top of each other and
place your finished cross stitch on top.
Stitch down the left-hand side to form a
book. If you wish, for added effect, you
could cut the edges of the felt with
pinking shears before you stitch them
together. Glue the ribbon over the seam
and secure it in a bow.

FORGET-ME-NOT

The forget-me-not is sometimes referred to as 'scorpion grass' because of the shape of the stem. Although there are no scorpions roaming wild in England, where the plant is mostly found, forget-me-nots are said to be a cure against the scorpion's sting. Another English name for this little plant is 'mouse ear' because of the shape of the woolly leaves.

According to Mrs Grieve, the plant has a strong affinity for the respiratory organs, especially the left lower lung. On the continent of Europe it used to be made into a syrup and given for pulmonary infections. There is a tradition that a decoction or juice of the plant hardens steel.

GERANIUM

In Victorian times geraniums were extremely popular, and they were grown in huge clumps in many a stately garden. The poor grew them too, but in pots on their window-sills. Nowadays, geraniums or, more correctly, pelargoniums are grown in dozens of different varieties, although the bright red flowers, said in the last century to resemble the brightly coloured uniforms of Queen Victoria's guards, are still among the most widely grown.

The word geranium comes from the Greek *geranos* (a crane), and the wild species is called crane's bill, from the resemblance of the fruit to the bill of the crane. The Turks say that this was a common mallow, changed to red by the touch of Mohammed's garment.

The leaves of some kinds of geranium can be used in jams and as flavouring for milk pudding. Other pelargoniums are cultivated for the distillation of a volatile oil from the leaves, which is not unlike that obtained from rose petals. *Pelargonium roseum* has very fragrant leaves, and *Pelargonium capitatum* yields pelargonic fatty acid.

In the language of flowers the red geranium means 'comforting'.

CYCLAMEN PILLOWCASE

This simple five-colour motif could be made more elaborate by increasing the number of pinks and mauves used to indicate the numerous colours of the flowers of the cyclamen. The curved design could be used on a blouse or a handbag, or it could be stitched vertically on the surround of a photograph frame.

The common name for this beautiful plant, sowbread, comes from the fact that the tuberous roots were once used as food for wild swine. Although the roots were a favourite food of swine, their juice is said to be poisonous to fish. Old writers tell us that cyclamen, baked and made into little flat cakes, has the reputation of being 'a good amorous medicine', causing the partaker to fall violently in love.

Long before it became popular as an indoor and greenhouse plant, cyclamen was valued as a medicinal root. It was used as a purgative and an emetic and as an antidote to poison. Because its leaves are shaped rather like the human ear, it was considered efficacious in diseases of that organ. The *Herbarium* of Apuleius relates that if a man's hair began to fall out he could avoid further loss by putting the herb up his nostrils. Its most valued medicinal property, however, was that it helped to make childbirth easy. Its powers in this direction were thought to be so great that in the sixteenth century pregnant women were warned to avoid places where it grew lest, by treading on it accidentally, they might bring on a miscarriage. Indeed, Gerard made a fence of sticks around the plants and laid others crosswise over them 'lest any woman should by lamentable experience' find this superstition to be true.

The name cyclamen comes from the Greek *kyklos* (circular). Some say this refers to the shape of the individual petals, others to the bulb-like root. Another suggestion is that it was so named because the flower stalks twist into spirals after flowering. In the language of flowers cyclamen is held to represent 'diffidence'.

Almost a hundred years ago a cyclamen was presented at a meeting of the Floral Committee of the Royal Horticultural Society. It had at least five hundred blossoms and was over seven years old, with a corm described as being 'nearly as large as a baby's head.' Some smaller varieties have been known to live for up to a hundred years.

There are many varieties of cyclamen available today, and while it is widely used as an indoor pot plant, there are miniature varieties that can be grown outdoors. An additional advantage of the plant is that you can choose the flowering time, for there are spring-, summer- and autumn- flowering varieties available. Cyclamens require well-drained rich soil and thrive best in partial shade. They can be grown from seed sown under glass in summer.

COMMON NAME: sowbread.

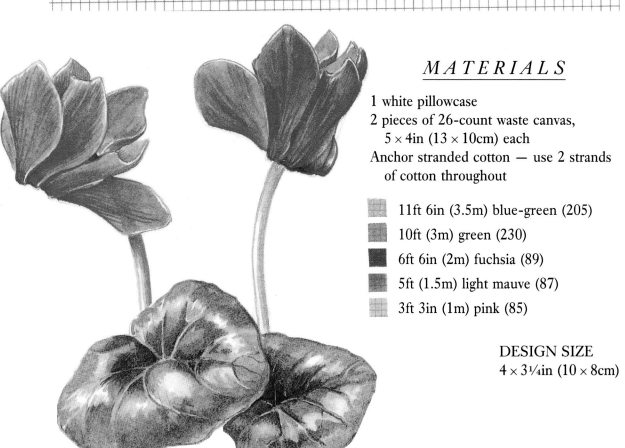

MATERIALS

1 white pillowcase
2 pieces of 26-count waste canvas,
  5 × 4in (13 × 10cm) each
Anchor stranded cotton — use 2 strands
  of cotton throughout

▨	11ft 6in (3.5m) blue-green (205)
▨	10ft (3m) green (230)
■	6ft 6in (2m) fuchsia (89)
▨	5ft (1.5m) light mauve (87)
▨	3ft 3in (1m) pink (85)

DESIGN SIZE
4 × 3¼in (10 × 8cm)

METHOD

Open out the pillowcase horizontally. Pin the pieces of waste canvas in position – i.e., one piece at the bottom left-hand corner and the other at the top right-hand corner and both approximately 3in (7.5cm) in from each edge. Tack (baste) the canvas in place. Starting with the bottom left-hand motif, begin following the chart from the top left-hand leaf, working in cross stitch with two strands of cotton and working over two strands of waste canvas both vertically and horizontally. When this motif is completed, turn the pillowcase around and repeat the motif in the opposite corner. Work the stems in fuchsia using small backstitch. Dampen with cold water and carefully pull out the strands of waste canvas from under the finished work.

If you do not like using waste canvas, you can trace the designs with a water-erasable pencil and transfer them on to the pillowcase before you begin.

FUCHSIA GREETINGS CARD

This simple motif can be repeated to form a border, used as a single spray on a hanky or a greetings card, or worked as two mirror images on either side of a photograph frame. It would also look pretty on the pocket of a shirt.

In the wild, the fuchsia, which is also known as lady's eardrops, is found in the Andes, from Colombia and Venezuela to Tierra del Fuego, in Hispaniola and in Brazil, Mexico and Central America. There is also a group of fuchsias that is native to New Zealand and Tahiti. Father Charles Plumier, a botanist and missionary, discovered the genus in Haiti in 1689–97, and he named it after the eminent professor of medicine, Leonhard Fuchs. Plumier called his new find *Fuchsia triphylla*, but the first species to arrive in England was a native of Brazil, *F. coccinea*. Tradition has it that it was introduced to Britain by a sailor, who arrived with it in the late eighteenth century and gave it to his wife, who kept the plant on a window-sill of their cottage in London's docklands. There, in 1788, the unusual flowers attracted the attention of nurseryman James Lee, who happened to be passing. He saw the potential of the plant and offered to buy it. After much haggling – the lady of the house struck a hard bargain – Lee paid the then massive sum of 80 guineas for the plant, but only on the condition that he provided her with a rooted cutting. By 1793 Lee had propagated sufficient stocks for general sale, and he was able to give the original owner three, selling the rest for a handsome profit.

Some fifty years after this, Messrs Veitch of Exeter caused something of a stir when they obtained the first flowering plants of yet another species from seeds they had obtained from Peru, where the plant had been discovered flowering in the Andes at an elevation of between 4,000 and 5,000 feet (1,200–1,500m).

These beautiful plants, with their bell-shaped heads and glorious colours, are now a common sight in our gardens. Some varieties are hardy, and even non-hardy plants can be overwintered with care.

In the language of flowers fuchsia represents 'taste'.

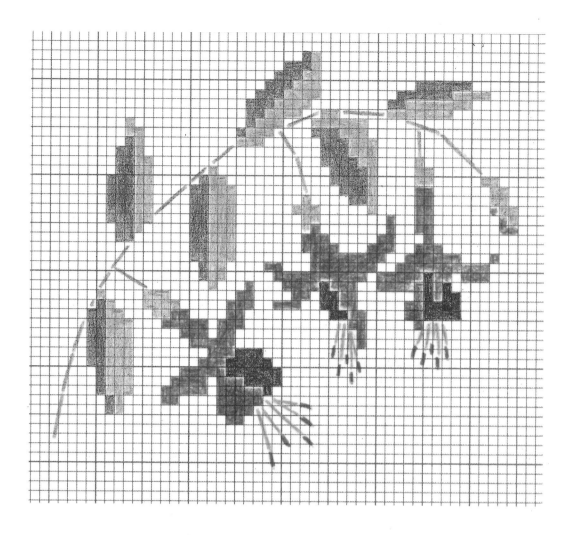

MATERIALS

1 piece of light-weight cotton fabric,
   7 × 5in (17.5 × 13cm)
1 piece of 26-count waste canvas, 4 × 3in
   (10 × 7.5cm)
5in (13cm) of 1½in (4cm) white lace
1 greetings card blank with oblong
   opening measuring 5¾ × 3¾in
   (14.5 × 9.5cm)
Rubber-based adhesive or adhesive tape
Anchor stranded cotton – use 2 strands
   throughout

- 20in (50cm) fuchsia (57)
- 20in (50cm) lavender (110)
- 20in (50cm) pink (25)
- 20in (50cm) green (923)
- 20in (50cm) olive green (862)
- 2in (5cm) coral (10)

METHOD

Tack (baste) the waste canvas into position
in the centre of the fabric. Fold the
material in half and then in half again to
find the centre. Mark the centre of the
chart and work outwards from that point.
Stitch using two strands of cotton and
working the crosses over two strands of
waste canvas both vertically and
horizontally. Work the stems and stamens
in small backstitch. When the chart is
complete, dampen your work with cold
water and carefully pull out the strands of
waste canvas from under the stitches.
Steam press on the wrong side of the work
over a towel. Sew the lace to the top edge
of the work and stick it into the card using
rubber-based adhesive or adhesive tape.

DESIGN SIZE
3¼ × 3in (8 × 7.5cm)

HOLLYHOCK MIRROR FRAME

This mirror image is worked in two colourways; it is ideal for a picture or mirror frame. Alternatively, you could work just one side of the design on table linen or to make a framed picture.

The stately hollyhock takes its botanic name *Althaea rosa* from the Greek word for 'cure' in reference to the healing properties of many of the species. This plant is native to Syria and is believed to be the 'holy mallow', discovered by crusaders who brought it back to Europe. It has been cultivated in Britain for more than five hundred years. The word hollyhock – 'holy hoc' – means holy great one.

Medicinally it serves as a substitute for the common mallow. Herbalists used the root of the plant, dried and powdered in wine, to kill worms in children, disperse blood clots, help ruptures and prevent miscarriages. Culpeper advised that 'the root is very binding and may be used to advantage,

both inwardly and outwardly, for incontinence of urine, immoderate menses, bleeding wounds, spitting of blood, the bloody flux and other fluxes of the belly'.

Mrs Grieve tells us that the flowers were also used for colouring purposes. 'They were sold freed from the calyx and were gathered in July and early August . . . and dried in trays, in thin layers, in a current of warm air.' Jean Palaiseul remarks that the 'dark purple flowers can be used to colour wine, but today, alas, chemical colouring matter is preferred'.

The hollyhock is the birthday flower for 25 June. It symbolizes ambition, fecundity and fruitfulness; the white hollyhock symbolizes female ambition.

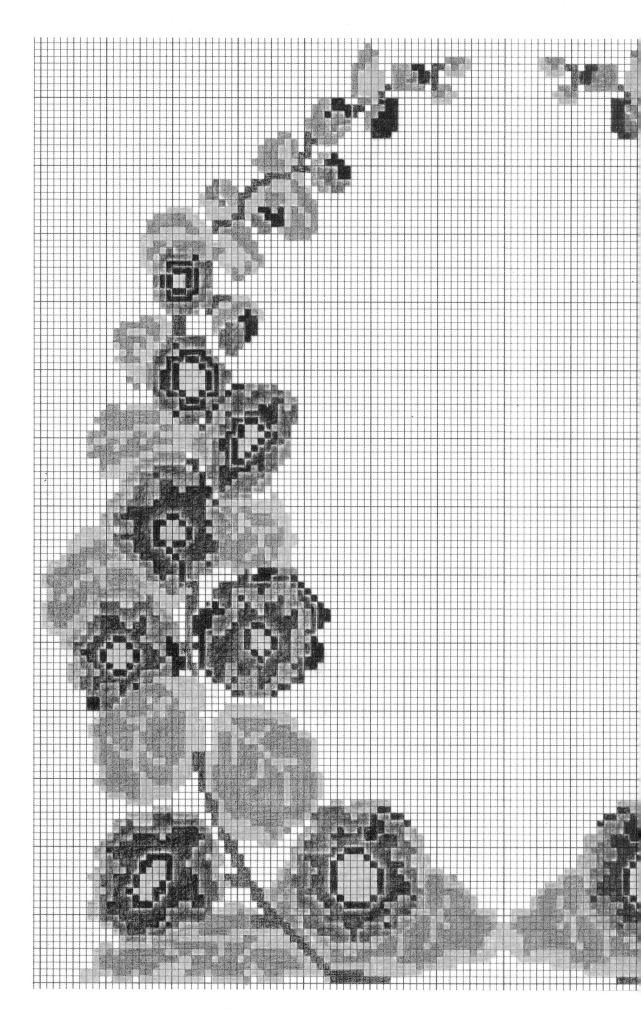

MATERIALS

1 piece of 14-count cream Aida,
  14 × 13in (36 × 33cm)
1 piece of heavy-duty cardboard,
  11 × 10½in (28 × 27cm)
1 piece of light-weight cardboard,
  11 × 10½in (28 × 27cm)
Craft knife
1 mirror, approximately 7 × 4in
  (17.5 × 10cm)
Rubber-based adhesive
Anchor stranded cotton – use 3 strands
  throughout

24ft 8in (7.5m) green (258)

13ft (4m) wine (897)

11ft 6in (3.5m) light green (255)

3ft 3in (1m) yellow (298)

3ft 3in (1m) moss green (681)

Left-hand side

18ft (5.5m) dark fuchsia (89)

18ft (5.5m) fuchsia (87)

10ft (3m) pink (85)

Right-hand side

18ft (5.5m) cherry (19)

18ft (5.5m) coral (11)

18ft (5.5m) pinky-red (57)

DESIGN SIZE
10½ × 10¼in (27 × 26cm)

To make a bath for Melancholy
Take Mallowes, pellitory of the wall, of each three
handfulls; Camomell flowers, Mellilot flowers, of
each one handfull; hollyhocks, two handfulls; Isop
one greate handfull, senerick seeds one ounce, and
boil them in nine gallon of Water until they come
to three, then put in a quart of new milke and go
into it bloud warm or something warmer.
ARCANA FAIRFAXIANA

METHOD

Fold the Aida in half and then in half again to find the centre. Mark the centre point on the chart and count out to the left to find where you should begin. Follow the chart, working in cross stitch and using three strands of cotton throughout.

MAKING UP

Draw the desired shape of the mirror frame on the light-weight cardboard and draw an oblong 6 × 3in (15 × 7.5cm) in the centre of the shape. Use a craft knife to cut out this shape and the outline. Lay the cut-out shape on the wrong side of the completed embroidery and draw around the oblong shape so that the outline can be seen on the canvas. Mark the diagonals up to ½in (1cm) from the corners and join these points. Cut away the waste canvas in the centre, slit the corners neatly and fold back ½in (1cm) all round, gluing the canvas to the cardboard to keep it in position. Fold back, stretch and glue the canvas around the outer edge of the cardboard. Cut the heavy-weight cardboard to the same shape as the completed frame and glue the mirror in the centre. Glue the mounted canvas to the piece of heavy-weight cardboard.

LILAC POUCH

This pretty pouch is worked on fine linen using shaded cotton. It is a beautiful motif that you could use on bed or table linen to bring spring into every room.

In the language of flowers the lilac represents the first emotion of love. White lilac is the symbol of purity, modesty and youth.

Lilac, *Syringa*, is a member of the olive family, and its botanic name derives from the Greek *surigx* (a tube or pipe). The plant used, in fact, to be known as blue-pipe because the hollow stems were used for pipes. Another popular name for the plant is oysters, although the origin is unclear, while in Devon the flowers are known as ducks' bills, no doubt because of the shape of the flower head.

Some country folk are superstitious about bringing lilac blooms indoors. The white varieties in particular are associated with death, and trees are said to refuse to bloom if another lilac tree in the same garden is cut down.

John Gerard thought the lilac had:

. . . a pleasante and sweete smell, but in my judgement too sweete, troubling and molesting the head in a very strange manner. I once gathered the flowers [of the common white lilac] and laid them in my chamber windowe, which smelled more strongly after they had been together a few howers, with such a ponticke and unacquainted savour, that they awaked me from sleepe, so that I could not take any rest till I had cast them out of my chamber. . . . [the scent of the purple lilac is] an exceeding sweet savour and scent but not so strong as the former: the flowers are of an exceeding faire blewe colour, compacted of many small flowers, in the forme of a bunche of grapes.

Nostalgia is a characteristic frequently associated with lilac, probably because of the heavy scent, which is often used in toiletries and perfumes. Lilac is also used in winemaking.

In some places finding a branch of lilac is supposed to signify a broken engagement. This theory was disproved in my own family on the day my father proposed marriage to my mother – he arrived on her doorstep with his arms full of bunches of white lilac. It is quite possible that, without the heavy scent of the flowers, this book would never have been written!

I remember, I remember,
The roses, red and white,
The vi'lets, and the lily-cups,
Those flowers made of light!
The lilacs where the robin built,
And where my brother set
The laburnum on his birthday, —
The tree is living yet.

I REMEMBER, *THOMAS HOOD (1799–1845)*

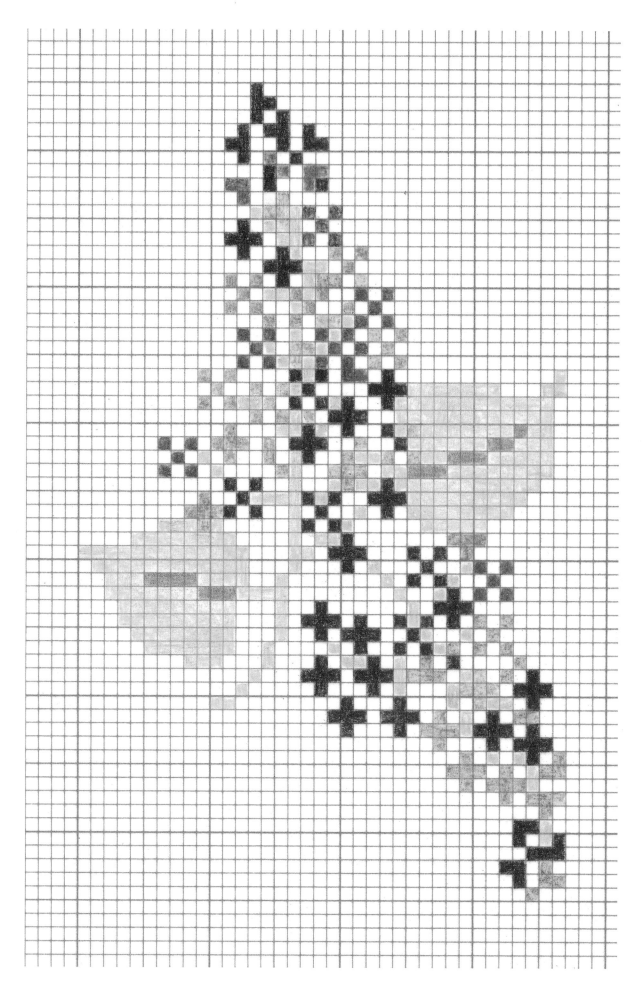

MATERIALS

1 piece of Irish linen, 10 × 6in
  (25 × 15cm)
1 piece of 26-count waste canvas,
  5 × 3½in (13 × 9cm)
Polyester wadding (batting)
Anchor stranded cotton – use 2 strands
  throughout

■ 26ft (8m) shaded lilac (1209)
■ 26ft (8m) shaded lilac (1209)
▦ 26ft (8m) shaded lilac (1209)
▦ 8ft 6in (2.5m) pale green (255)
▦ 20in (50cm) green (265)

METHOD

Lay the linen in front of you vertically
and tack (baste) waste canvas in position
horizontally across the centre. Fold the
linen and canvas in half and then in half
again to find the centre. Mark the centre
stitch on the chart and work outwards
from this point. Divide the shaded cotton
roughly into dark and light strands and
stitch, using two strands of cotton and
working across two strands of waste
canvas both vertically and horizontally.
Follow the chart in cross stitch
throughout.

MAKING UP

When the needlepoint is complete, fold
back and hem the two long edges. Fold
two or three thicknesses of wadding
(batting) to form an oblong 5½ × 4in
(14 × 10cm) and place this behind the
design, sprinkling it with a couple of
drops of perfumed essence. Fold the two
short ends in to the centre and join at the
centre back. Join the side seams,
oversewing in buttonhole stitch (see
Techniques) and using three strands of
the darkest shade of lilac cotton.

DESIGN SIZE
4½ × 3in (11 × 7.5cm)

LILY-OF-THE-VALLEY PHOTOGRAPH ALBUM

Repeat patterns of whitework make a pleasing border, and they can be worked on any fabric to achieve a strong contrast or a subtle difference. This panel could be repeated two or three times along a runner or used as a table mat.

The lily-of-the-valley, *Convallaria majalis*, was cultivated in English gardens in the seventeenth century. Culpeper (1616–54) reported that in his time these little lilies grew plentifully on Hampstead Heath, but Green, writing in the 1830s, reported that 'since the trees on Hampstead Heath, near London, have been destroyed, [they] have been but sparingly found there'.

Lily-of-the-valley signifies the virtues of purity and humility, and in the language of flowers it means 'return of happiness'.

In the Middle Ages the flower was considered an important ingredient in love potions, and it is still said that a sprig of lily-of-the-valley can help to mend a broken heart. According to legend, the fragrance of the flowers draws the nightingale from the hedge and bush and leads him to choose his mate in the recesses of the glade.

In *English Physician and Complete Herbal* Culpeper says that the distilled water of the flowers 'comforts the heart and vital spirits', restores the power of

speech when it has been lost, helps in cases of palsy and is 'excellently good in the apoplexy'. He also recommends the plant for a failing memory and inflammation of the eyes.

In spite of their innocent appearance and sweet scent, lilies-of-the-valley are sometimes thought to be ill-omened, probably because they are white and have hanging heads. Thistleton Dyer, writing in the 1880s, mentions a Westcountry belief that it is dangerous to plant a bed of these flowers in the garden. Whoever does so will die within a year.

In Norway a spirit made of lilies-of-the-valley was drunk as a 'dram' and could also be used to flavour puddings and cakes. The recipe was given in *The Country Lady's Director* (1732):

Gather your Lily-of-the-Valley Flowers, when they are dry, and pick them from the Stalks; then put a Quarter of a Pint of them into a Quart of Brandy, and so in proportion, to infuse six or eight Days; then distil it in a cold still, marking the Bottles, as they are drawn off, which is first, second, and third, etc. When you have distill'd them, take the first, and so on to the third and fourth and mix them together, till you have as strong as you desire; and then bottle them and cork them well, putting a lump of Loaf-Sugar into each Bottle.

COMMON NAMES: May lily, May flower, Our Lady's tears, convall-lily, lily constancy, ladder-to-heaven, liriconfancy, Jacob's ladder, male lily, little May bells (Germany).

MATERIALS

1 piece of 27-count Linda, 26 × 17in (66 × 43cm) or to fit your album with a 3in (7.5cm) allowance all around
1 photograph album, 13 × 11in (33 × 28cm)
Rubber-based adhesive
2 pieces of felt or coloured paper, 13 × 11in (33 × 28cm) each
1yd (1m) white cord
Anchor stranded cotton – use 2 strands throughout
78ft (24m – 3 skeins) white (1)

METHOD

Fold the fabric in half horizontally. Measure the width of the spine of your album and if it is, say, 2in (5cm) mark a vertical chalk line 1in (2.5cm) – i.e., half the width of the spine – in from your crease and fold the fabric vertically down this line. You will be working the design on half the width of the canvas, so fold it again, horizontally and vertically and taking the 1in (2.5cm) into account, to find the centre. Mark the centre of the chart and work outwards from this point, using two strands of thread and working the crosses over two strands of Linda, both vertically and horizontally. Work the complete design in cross stitch.

MAKING UP

Lay the completed design face down in front of you with the open album centred on top. Carefully make two cuts 3in (7.5cm) deep on either side of the spine at the top and the bottom. Fold these flaps into the spine, gluing them in position. Fold over the fabric at the top and bottom edges of the front and back and glue it down. Repeat at the two long edges. Trim the felt or coloured paper to fit inside the cover and glue on top over the raw edges. Thread the cord through the spine and fasten with a knot.

DESIGN SIZE
8 × 7½in (20 × 19cm)

The Naiad-like Lily of the Vale
Whom youth makes so fair and passion so pale,
That the light of its tremulous bells is seen
Through their pavilions of tender green.
PERCY BYSSHE SHELLEY (1792–1822)

MARIGOLD PILLOWCASE

There is nothing prettier than white bedding piled high with embroidered white linen cushions. You can make them up in all shapes and sizes, and trim them as you please. This pretty marigold design is stitched onto a baby's pillowcase, which I bought already trimmed with broderie anglaise. You could, of course, use the design on any number of items as a corner motif.

The marigold, *Calendula officinalis*, was once widely used as a kitchen herb. It was often planted in or near to the vegetable garden in the belief that it would deter insect pests from attacking the other plants, and the flower head rubbed on a wasp- or bee-sting was said to cure the pain immediately. The petals were sometimes used as a cheap substitute for saffron and used to colour cheese, and the flowers add a rich, cheesy flavour to salads.

Like other plants with yellow petals it served as a protection against witchcraft, and the French king Jean d'Aragon, acting on the advice of Spanish sorcerers, advised his subjects to wear as a talisman a marigold, picked when the sun was entering the sign of the Virgin, wrapped together with a wolf's tooth in a bay leaf. To dream of marigold flowers in full bloom was considered a certain sign of coming wealth.

The marigold was well known to the old herbalists. Fuller, in his *Antheologie* (1655), wrote: 'We all know the many and sovereign virtues in your leaves, the Herbe Generalle in all pottage'. And Stevens, in *Maison Rustique, or the Countrie Farme* (1699), mentions the marigold as a specific for headache,

jaundice, red eyes, toothache and ague. The physicians of Myddfai offerd an early Celtic remedy for typhus fever:

Take marigold, pound well with good wine, vinegar, strong mead, or strong old ale. Strain carefully, and drink a good draught in the morning fasting, whilst the pestilence lasts. If you are taken ill, you need no other than this as your only drink. It is a good preservative against the foreign pestilence, called the plague.

The African marigold began life as a Mexican wild flower, and it takes its botanical name from *Calends* (the root of the English word calendar) because the early species appeared to flower on the first day of each Roman calendar month. The cultivated marigold flowers throughout summer to early autumn and thrives best in poor soil in sun or partial shade.

The marigold is often associated with grief, but it also has close links with the sun. It opens its petals in the morning, follows the sun across the sky and closes its petals in the afternoon. This closing of the petals was said by the ancient poets to be an expression of mourning for the sun. In southeast Europe a magical method of ensuring a lover's faithfulness was to dig earth secretly from his footprints, put it in a pot and sow marigold seeds therein. If a man looked long and carefully into the flowers first thing in the morning, he was deemed to be safe from contagion throughout the whole of that day.

In southern Europe marigolds were dedicated to the Virgin Mary, and in England during the seventeenth century they were associated with Queen Mary.

A posy of marigolds and roses was a traditional emblem of the sweet sorrows of love. Joined with other flowers, marigolds are said to represent the varying course of life between good and ill. In the east a bouquet of marigolds and poppies means 'I will soothe your grief'. In the language of flowers the marigold means 'grief, pain or chagrin'.

COMMON NAMES: golds, ruddes, Mary Gowles, Oculus Christi, pot marigold, marygold, fiore d'ogni mese (Italy), solis sponsa, husbandman's dial, summer's bride.

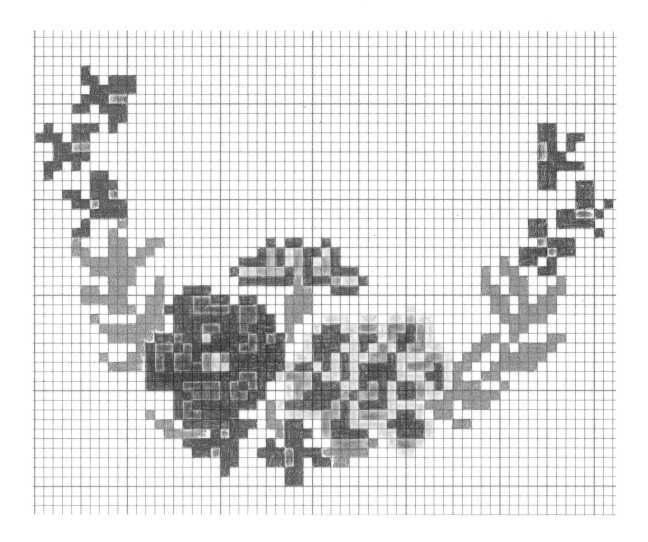

MATERIALS

1 small white cotton pillowcase
1 piece of 26-count waste canvas, 5 × 4in
(13 × 10cm)
Broderie anglaise trim to fit around outer
edges
Anchor stranded cotton – use 2 strands
throughout

▨ 5ft (1.5m) orange (925)

▨ 5ft (1.5m) green (227)

▨ 3ft 3in (1m) yellow (298)

▨ 3ft 3in (1m) blue (147)

▨ 20in (50cm) red (334)

▨ 20in (50cm) gold (304)

▨ 20in (50cm) silver (274)

DESIGN SIZE
4½ × 3¼in (11 × 8cm)

METHOD

Position the waste canvas in the centre of
the pillowcase, 2in (5cm) in from the
short end, and tack (baste) it in position.
Find the centre of the chart and work
outwards from this point, stitching with
two strands of cotton and working
crosses over two strands of canvas both
vertically and horizontally. When the
design is complete, dampen the
embroidery with cold water and carefully
remove the waste canvas.

Sew the broderie anglaise edging
neatly around the pillowcase, adding
ribbons or bows as you wish.

MEADOW FLOWER TABLE-CLOTH

These pretty squares of linen are decorated with sprays of honeysuckle, poppies, clover and forget-me-nots – some of the loveliest flowers of the meadows and woodlands. The panels are joined with insertion lace, so you can make the cloth as large or as small as you wish. You could also make napkins to match, decorating a corner with a motif from the main design.

HONEYSUCKLE

Described by the diarist Samuel Pepys as 'the trumpet flower' whose bugles 'blow scent instead of sound', honeysuckle, *Lonicera periclymenum*, symbolizes sweetness of disposition, bonds of love and domestic happiness. It has always been the symbol of faithful love, Chaucer telling us that those who

> Wore chapelets on hir hede
> Of fresh wodebind, be such as never
> were
> To love untrue, in word ne thought,
> ne dede,
> But ay steadfast: ne for pleasance, ne
> fere
> Tho' that they shoulde hir hertes all
> to tere,
> Would never flit, but ever were
> stedfast
> Till that hir lives theie asunder brust.

Woodbine, as honeysuckle is also known, was one of Shakespeare's favourite flowers – in *A Midsummer Night's Dream* Titania sleeps on a bank 'quite over-canopied with luscious woodbine' – and in *Lycidas* Milton writes of the 'well-attir'd woodbine'.

Come into the garden, Maud,
For the black bat, night, has flown;
Come into the garden, Maud,
I am here at the gate alone;
And the woodbine spices
are wafted abroad,
And the musk of the rose is blown.

MAUD,
ALFRED, LORD TENNYSON (1809–92)

The herbalists found uses for the plant. Waller tells us: 'a decoction of the flowers has been celebrated as an excellent antispasmodic and recommended in asthama of the nervous kind. An elegant water may be distilled from these flowers, which has been recommended for nervous headache.' Culpeper wrote:

It is a plant so common that everyone that hath eyes know it, and he that hath none, cannot read a description if I should write it. . . . What is it good for? It is good for something, for God and nature made nothing in vain. It is a herb of Mercury, and appropriated to the lungs; the celestial Crab claims dominion over it, neither is it a foe of the Lion; if the lungs be afflicted by Jupiter, this is your cure. It is fitting a conserve made of the flowers should be kept in every gentlewoman's house; . . . Authors say, the flowers are of more effect than the leaves, and that is true, but they say the seeds are the least effectual of all. But Dr Reason told me, There is a vital spirit in every seed to beget its like; and Dr Experience told me, There is a greater heat in the seed than in any other part of the plant; and heat is the mother of action.

COMMON NAMES: woodbine, goats' leaf, chèvre-feuille (France), Geisblatt (Germany), capri-foglio (Italy).

POPPY

The red poppy, *Papaver rhoeas*, no longer fills our meadows in the summer, but the blaze of red can still be seen along the edges of meadows and on road-side verges. An ancient Greek legend says it was created by Somnus, the god of sleep, to give to Ceres, the corn goddess, when she was so wearied by the search for her lost daughter, Proserpine (Persephone), that she could not make the corn grow. To save mankind from starvation, Somnus gave her poppies to make her sleep, and when she had rested her strength returned and the corn grew again.

The Greeks also associated poppies with fertility because of their many seeds, which were used to flavour food and given with wine and honey to athletes training for the Olympic Games. The ancient Egyptians made garlands of poppies (some have been found in tombs dating from the time of the Pharaohs) and used the seeds as a condiment.

Traditionally, a poppy was used to prove the sincerity of affection between lovers. A petal of the flower was placed in the left hand and struck with the right hand. If a snapping sound was heard, the holder was considered sincere.

In folk medicine poppy heads were often used to cure earache, toothache and so forth, and warmed leaves were laid against the face to cure neuralgia.

In spite of these virtues, poppies are often considered to be ill-omened flowers. In Oxfordshire, for example, it is said to be unlucky to bring poppies indoors, and some say it is better not to pick them at all. Children almost everywhere say that if anyone looks into the flower's heart, he or she will go blind, if only temporarily. In Yorkshire it is sometimes called blind buff for this reason. The flowers are also said to cause violent earache if they are held against the ear.

Like waterlilies, poppies used to be considered a potent remedy against the passion of love, and they were used for this purpose in both magic and medicine.

COMMON NAMES: corn rose, corn poppy, flores rhoeados, headache.

CLOVER

The delicate scent of red clover, *Trifolium pratense*, attracts bees, butterflies and moths – in fact, the plant is sometimes known as bee bread so many insects are drawn to it. In country districts the flowers were made into a potent wine and into a syrup for the relief of whooping cough.

Clover was one of the plants that protected humans and animals from the spells of magicians and witches and against the wiles of fairies. It was also thought to bring good fortune to those who kept it in the home or wore it in their buttonholes or hats. Although all clover has magical properties, the rare, four-leaved kind was held to be especially powerful. The finder of such a plant could see fairies, detect witches and recognize evil spirits. The plant could also be used in love divination. If a girl wore such a leaf in her right shoe the first man she met on her first journey with it would be her future husband, or, if not he, another man of the same name. To dream of clover was fortunate for young people, since such a dream foretold a happy and prosperous marriage.

COMMON NAMES: trefoil, bee bread.

FORGET-ME-NOT

In Italy the forget-me-not is the flower of love, and in France it is also a symbol of affection.

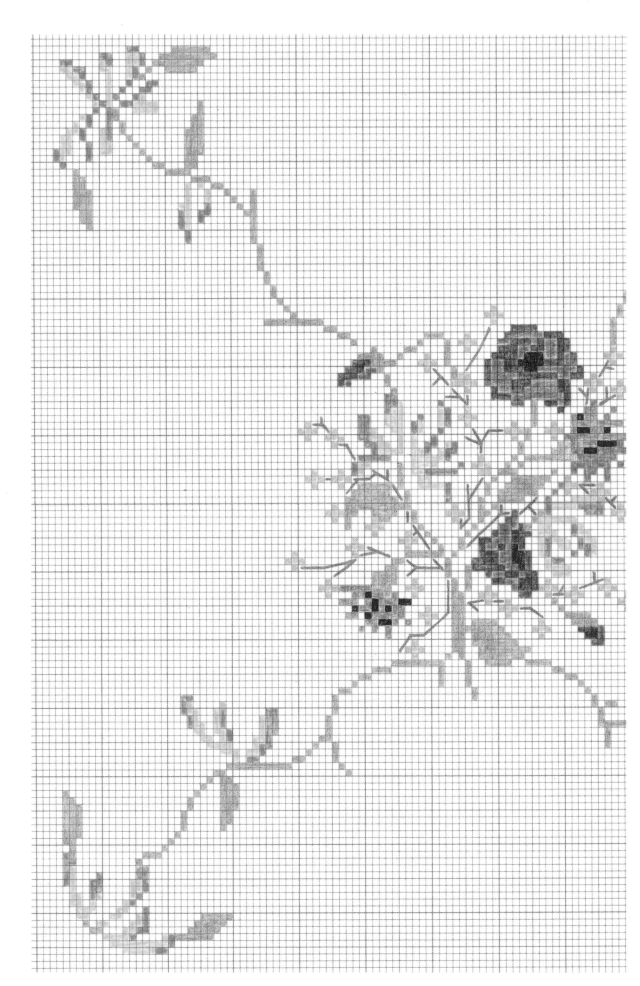

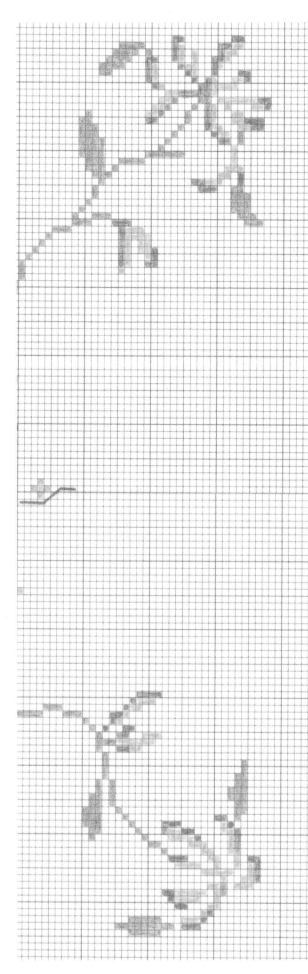

MATERIALS

9 (or number required) pieces of white
 Irish linen, 12 × 12in (30 × 30cm) each
9 (or number required) pieces of 26-
 count waste canvas, 10 × 10in
 (25 × 25cm) each
Approximately 33ft (10m) of insertion
 lace
Edging lace to fit around finished cloth
White sewing thread
Anchor stranded cotton (for each square)
 – use 2 strands throughout

11ft 6in (3.5m) green (256)

6ft 6in (2m) yellow (305)

6ft 6in (2m) peach (4146)

3ft 3in (1m) blue (117)

3ft 3in (1m) red (335)

3ft 3in (1m) dark pink (28)

20in (50cm) mauve (97)

20in (50cm) dark mauve (99)

20in (50cm) chocolate (382)

20in (50cm) olive green (846)

DESIGN SIZE
9½ × 9in (24 × 23cm)

METHOD

Centre a piece of waste canvas on a
square of linen and pin, then tack (baste)
it in position. Find the centre by folding
the fabric in half and then in half again.
Mark the centre of the chart and work
outwards from this point. Stitch using
two strands of cotton and working
crosses over two strands of waste canvas
both vertically and horizontally. Work the
stem details in olive green, using two
strands of cotton and in a small
backstitch. When the design is complete,
dampen the fabric and carefully remove
the waste canvas.

MAKING UP

When your squares are complete, either
roll and hand hem the edges or, using a
sewing machine, secure the raw edges
with zigzag stitch then turn them back
and use a very small straight stitch to
hem them. Lay the squares on a table. If
you are using lace that is 2in (5cm) wide,
leave 2in (5cm) between each square.
The table cloth illustrated here is three
squares wide and three squares deep, so
I cut eight lengths of lace to fit from
edge to edge both vertically and
horizontally, allowing for the width of
lace between – that is, three squares,
each 11½in (29cm) deep, plus the width
of two lace inserts, each 2in (5cm) deep,
so that each piece of lace was 38½in
(97cm) long. Hand sew the lace into
position on top of the edges of the
squares, overlapping the lace where the
strips cross. Neatly sew edging lace all
around the finished cloth, taking care to
secure the raw ends of the lace inserts.

O you poor folk in cities
A thousand, thousand pities!
Heaping the fairy gold that withers and dies;
One field in the June weather
Is worth all the gold ye gather,
One field in June weather — one Paradise.
  KATHERINE TYNAN

Summer set lip to earth's Bosom bare,
And left the flushed print in a poppy there;
Like a yawn of fire from the grass it came,
And the fanning wind puffed it to flapping flame.
THE POPPY (TO MONICA), *FRANCIS THOMPSON*
1859–1907

Pansy Address Book Cover and Cushion

The pansy is grown in so many colour variations that it was difficult to make a choice for this design. Do not feel that you should slavishly follow the colours shown – mix and match them as you wish and work the design on any colour background you choose.

The pansy, *Viola × wittrockiana*, has been developed from the violet, and the little spots that can be seen clearly in the white violet have been enlarged through hybridizing and cultivation until they have become the markings that now so strangely suggest a face.

The name pansy is derived from the French word *pensée* (a thought). Numerous spellings can be found in old poetry – panses, penses, paunces, pancyes and pawnces – and there can be few plants with so many other curious names – ladies' flower, bird's eye, pink of my John, Kit run in the street, flamy, cull me, call me, stepmother, sister in law, the longer the dearer, kiss me quick, kiss me at the garden gate, cuddle me, jump up and kiss me and kiss me ere I rise!

The plant was a great favourite of Victorian gardeners, and in 1813 Lord Gambier, from Iver, Buckinghamshire, and his gardener, Thomson, cultivated and improved them, eventually naming one variety 'Queen Victoria'.

There's rosemary,
that's for remembrance;
pray, love, remember:
and there is pansies,
that's for thoughts.
HAMLET,
WILLIAM SHAKESPEARE (1564–1616)

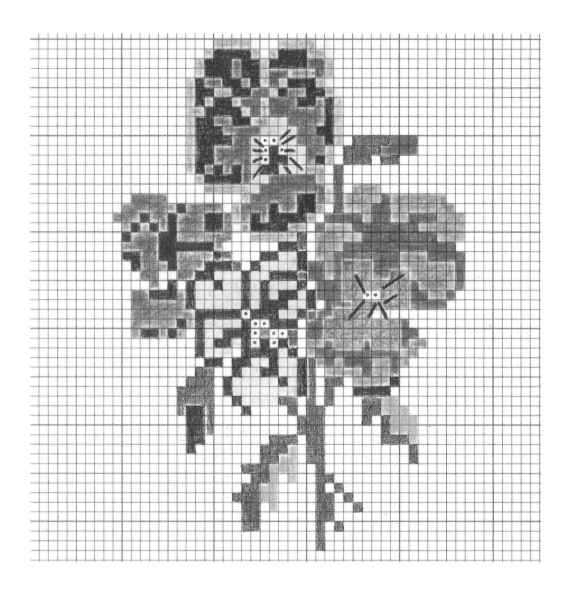

MATERIALS

Address book

1 piece of 30-count tea-coloured linen,
   14 × 10in (36 × 25cm) or to fit your
   address book with a 5in (13cm)
   allowance widthways and a 3in (7.5)
   allowance lengthways

Rubber-based adhesive

Cushion

1 piece of 26-count cream linen, 8 × 7in
   (20 × 17.5cm)

1 piece of cotton backing, 8 × 7in
   (20 × 17.5cm)

20in (50cm) of broderie anglaise eyelet
   trim

30in (75cm) narrow green satin ribbon

Polyester wadding (batting)

Anchor stranded cotton – use 2 strands
   of cotton throughout

3ft 3in (1m) mauve (92)

3ft 3in (1m) dark mauve (94)

3ft 3in (1m) gold (298)

3ft 3in (1m) wine (22)

3ft 3in (1m) rust (326)

3ft 3in (1m) orange (925)

3ft 3in (1m) green (923)

20in (50cm) lilac (90)

20in (50cm) purple (101)

20in (50cm) white (1)

20in (50cm) blue-green (205)

DESIGN SIZE

Address book – 3½ × 2½in (9 × 6.5cm);
cushion – 4¼ × 3in (10.5 × 7.5cm)

I send thee Pansies while the year is young,
Yellow as sunshine, purple as the night;
Flowers of remembrance, ever fondly sung
By all the chiefest of the sons of light;
And if in recollection lives regret
For wasted days, and dreams that were not true,
I tell thee that the pansy 'freaked with jet'
Is still with the heart's-ease that the poets knew.
Take all the sweetness of a gift unsought,
And for the pansies send me back a thought.
SARAH DOUDNEY (1843–1926)

CUSHION

METHOD

Fold the linen in half and then in half again to find the centre. Mark the centre of the chart and work outwards from this point. Stitch using two strands of cotton, working crosses over two strands of linen both vertically and horizontally. Follow the chart in cross stitch but work the details at the centre of the flowers in wine using small straight stitches.

MAKING UP

Lay the completed work on top of the cotton backing so that the wrong sides are facing. Turn in all the edges and insert the trim. Pin and carefully sew together, filling with the wadding (batting). If you wish, add a drop of perfumed essence to the wadding (batting). Thread the ribbon in and out of the eyelets and secure it with a small bow at one corner.

ADDRESS BOOK

M E T H O D

Fold and crease the linen in half lengthwise over the address book, allowing 2½in (6cm) at each end to fold back inside the book cover. Fold the linen in half widthways to find the centre point on the right-hand side (the front of the book cover). Mark the centre of the chart and work outwards from this point. Stitch, using two strands of cotton and working across over two strands of linen both vertically and horizontally. Follow the chart in cross stitch but work the detail at the flower centres with small straight stitches in wine.

M A K I N G   U P

Open the book and place the finished work in position over it. Make sure that you allow for the movement of opening and closing the book, then glue the flaps down to the inside of the cover. Cut two small slits either side of the bottom and top of the spine of the book and brush the flaps with the adhesive. Use a knitting needle or paper knife to push the flaps into the spine. Fold up the bottom and top flaps on the front and back covers and glue them into place. Edge the linen with braid if you wish.

There is the house, with the gate red-barred,
And the poplars tall;
And the barn's brown length, and the cattle-yard,
And the white horns tossing above the wall.

There are the beehives ranged in the sun;
And down by the brink
Of the brook are her poor flowers, weed-o'errun,
Pansy and daffodil, rose and pink.
TELLING THE BEES
JOHN GREENLEAF WHITTIER (1807–92)

PARROT TULIP CUSHION

The tulip panel can be made up as a fancy frilly cushion or a simple backed square with a piped surround. The motifs could be used singly on other projects, and the colours you use are entirely up to you.

The tulip (*Tulipa*) was originally a wild flower in the Levant, whence it was brought to Europe by the crusaders. The name tulip comes from the Turkish *tuliband* or *toliband*, which was, in turn, derived from the Persian *dulband* (turban). There is a Persian

Here tulips bloom as they are told;
Unkempt about those hedges blows
An English unofficial rose.
THE OLD VICARAGE, GRANTCHESTER,
RUPERT BROOKE (1887–1915)

legend that the flower sprang from the blood of Farhad, who had thrown himself off a mountain when he heard a false rumour that his beloved, Shirin, had been killed. In Persia the tulip was the emblem of perfect love. In the language of flowers the variegated tulip means 'beautiful eyes', the yellow tulip means 'hopeless love', and the red tulip is a declaration of love.

Around 1554 the ambassador to Turkey from the court of the Emperor Ferdinand I of Austria was given some tulip bulbs as a gift when he returned to Vienna. Some twenty years later de l'Escluse (Clusius), a French professor of botany, was sent to the Netherlands from Vienna, and he took some bulbs with him, only to have them stolen. It seems that he was asking too much money for the bulbs, and the Dutch, who wanted to cultivate the flowers, were prepared to steal what they could not afford to buy. The tulip became the flower of rich landowners, and they competed with German growers to obtain the best bulbs from Turkey and the Levant.

In the 1630s tulip mania gripped Holland, and the bulbs became the source of manic speculation. Fights broke out, people were killed, and fortunes were made and lost. One variety called 'Viceroy' was sold for £250 and another, 'Semper Augustus', for more than double that amount. Finally, the government had to control the trading, which had become mere stock-jobbing speculation, with bulbs that had not even flowered changing hands at ever-increasing prices, and in 1637 the market collapsed, leaving many hundreds destitute. Today tulips are a major industry, filling hundreds of catalogues and attracting thousands of tourists.

MATERIALS

1 piece of 14-count navy blue Aida,
  13½ × 14½in (34.5 × 37cm)
1yd (1m) of red chintz
10in (25cm) of navy blue chintz
3yd (3m) of piping cord
1 cushion pad, 18in (45.5cm) in diameter
Anchor stranded cotton – use 2 strands
  throughout

- 21ft 6in (6.5m) olive green (267)
- 20ft (6m) green (255)
- 18ft (5.5m) yellow (298)
- 15ft (4.5m) mauve (92)
- 11ft 6in (3.5m) dark pink (27)
- 11ft 6in (3.5m) light pink (23)
- 11ft 6in (3.5m) red (334)
- 6ft 6in (2m) cherry (29)
- 3ft 3in (1m) orange (925)
- 20in (50cm) black (403)

DESIGN SIZE
12½ × 13½in (32 × 34.5cm)

METHOD

Fold the Aida in half and then in half again to find the centre. Mark the centre of the chart and work outwards from this point. Stitch using two strands of cotton throughout and working the entire pattern in cross stitch.

MAKING UP

Using a sewing machine and a small straight stitch, cover the piping cord with navy blue chintz. Cut two pieces of red chintz, 18 × 16in (46 × 41cm) each. Turn back the edges of the Aida by about ½in

(1cm), insert the piping around the edge of your design and stitch it to the centre of one of the pieces of red chintz.

Cut two strips of red chintz measuring approximately 64 × 3½in (162.5 × 9cm). Join them together into one long piece. Carefully hem one long end and stitch a row of running stitches along the other long edge. Gather the chintz evenly into a frill until it fits neatly around the cushion. Turn in all the edges of the red chintz pieces by ½in (1cm). Tack together the back pieces, the frill, the navy piping and then the front, leaving a space for a zipper if you wish. Machine or hand oversew carefully in place, joining the remaining short ends of the frill.

PRIMULA SEWING TIDY

This is the ideal project for cross stitch enthusiasts who have more cushions and pictures than they know what to do with. This little case, with its repeating motif, is the perfect way to keep your projects clean and accessible. You could, of course, expand on this idea and make a tidy in which to keep jewellery or your make-up.

The primula family is remarkable for the number of hybrids it produces. One of the favourite plants of cottage gardens is the polyanthus – Francis Thompson's 'polyanthus of unnumbered dyes' – and the family also includes cowslips, primroses, oxlips and auriculas.

The auricula arrived in our gardens in the sixteenth century, largely owing to the French botanist de l'Escluse (Clusius), to whom all tulip lovers owe so much. The Emperor Maximilian II was himself a great garden lover, and when de l'Escluse accepted the Emperor's invitation to become botanist at the Court of Vienna he was able to spend much time climbing in the Tyrol in search of fresh treasures. De l'Escluse sent roots of the auricula to his friend van de Delft in Belgium, and from there they spread, becoming established in English gardens by the early seventeenth century. Even before then, however, Gerard, in his *Herball*, which was published in 1596, called auriculas 'beare's eares' or 'mountain cowslips'. He laid great emphasis on the medicinal value of the plants:

> The Swiss called them 'Schwindledraut' and used the roots for strengthening of the head, so when they are on top of places that are high 'giddiness' and the swimming of the 'braine' may not affect them. . . . They does all call it Paralytica because of his virtues in curing the palsies, cramps and convulsions. The rootes . . . taking in the way of one or two drams, helpeth such as have devoured the Sea Hare, or have been bitten by a Toad, or taken too great a quantity of opium. . . . The Swiss eat rootes of Auriculas before climbing mountains to prevent loss of use of 'neckes'.

During the latter half of the seventeenth century auriculas developed into something of a cult, and in his *Florist's Vade Mecum* (1683), Samuel Gilbert stated that enthusiasts paid as much as £20 for a root.

All the hardy varieties of primula – primrose, cowslip, auricula and polyanthus – may be easily propagated by dividing the roots of established plants in autumn.

DESIGN SIZE
5 × 4½in (13 × 11cm)

MATERIALS

1 piece of 14-count cream Aida,
19 × 10in (48.5 × 25cm)
1 piece of cotton fabric, 22 × 11in
(56 × 28cm)
30in (75cm) of ½in (1cm) satin ribbon
Sewing thread
Anchor stranded cotton – use 2 strands
throughout

26ft (8m) green (256)

15ft (4.5m) pale green (254)

13ft (4m) gold (298)

11ft 6in (3.5m) cream (852)

5ft (1.5m) chocolate (382)

Colourway 1

6ft 6in (2m) maroon (22)

3ft 3in (1m) cerise (29)

Colourway 2

6ft 6in (2m) red (335)

3ft 3in (1m) orange (304)

Colourway 3

6ft 6in (2m) dark blue (119)

3ft 3in (1m) blue (118)

METHOD

Fold the Aida in half and then in half
again to find the centre. Mark the centre
of the chart and begin working outwards
from that point, stitching the central
motif in colourway 2. Use two strands of
cotton. Leave 1½in (4cm) between each
flower and repeat the motifs to the left
and right, using colourways 1 and 3
respectively.

MAKING UP

When the design is complete, turn back
and crease the Aida 1in (2.5cm) in along
the top and bottom edges and ½in (1cm)
in along the two short edges. Cut a piece
1in (2.5cm) wide from the long side of
the lining fabric and fold this in half,
with right sides together, to form a strip
½in (1cm) wide. Sew along the long
edge, then use a knitting needle to push
the fabric through the tube and turn it
the right way out. Fold in the top, bottom
and one of the side edges of the
remaining piece of lining fabric and use
small stitches to oversew it to the back of
the Aida, leaving a 3in (7.5cm) flap at the

left-hand edge and a small gap at the centre of each of the short ends to insert the ribbon. Turn the flap inwards and hem the raw edge of what was the left-hand short end. Carefully cut the fabric at the left-hand top and bottom corners of the Aida and turn in the fabric, stitching it down along the top and bottom edges.

Take the strip of fabric and place it approximately 3in (7.5cm) down on the right edge of your work (that is, on the opposite side to the flap). Stitch one of the short ends to the edge of the fabric and then make six loops of about 1in (2.5cm) – these will hold skeins of cotton – catching the fabric strip in place between each loop with small backstitches. Leave the next 3in (7.5cm) of fabric strip free, then secure it with another row of backstitch. Leave the remaining strip free and secure the end with small backstitches. You now have six spaces for cotton, a space for your yarn organizer and a space for your canvas together with a pocket for your chart.

Add a small pocket to the front of the chart flap to hold your sewing scissors and a small square of spare Aida for your needles. Cut the length of ribbon in two and insert an end of each piece into the gap you left at the centres of the short edges. Sew them securely in position.

ROSE ON LINEN

This book would not be complete without a framed picture of the queen of flowers. This motif would look just as attractive in the centre of a lace pillow or on a sachet filled with pot pourri.

In the language of flowers to give a rose is to say 'I love you'. The unopened rose signifies unawakened love; the full bloom means 'beauty at its fullest – but beauty must pass'. The pink rose is the flower of grace; the red rose is the flower of passion and ardour; the white rose symbolizes purity and spiritual love; the yellow rose means jealousy.

Roses have long been associated with cosmetics and beauty preparations. Rose oil used to be applied to lend a sheen to the eyelids and, in times when dental care was unheard of, pastilles made from myrrh and rose petals crushed in honey were chewed to sweeten the breath. In Elizabethan times rosewater was distilled from the petals and used for bathing. The first people to make medicinal use of the rose were the Arabs, among whom it was used as a specific for tuberculosis and pulmonary complaints. All manner of syrups, ointments and vinegars were produced from the flowers by herbalists, and there are numerous recipes for jams, sweets, soups, salads, jellies and drinks.

Roses played an important part in the feasts held in ancient Rome in honour of Bacchus, the god of wine – indeed, the Romans seem to have been obsessed by the rose, even using the flower to perfume their public baths and fountains. At banquets and orgies, roses were strewn about, and rose petals were used to stuff pillows and mattresses. Rose-filled sachets were steeped in wine to perfume it. Rose pudding was a delicacy, and if you were offered a love potion it would, of course, taste of roses. The flower came to epitomize the worst excesses of the Roman empire, with many peasants being forced to grow roses instead of food crops in order to satisfy the hedonistic demands of their rulers.

The early popes refused to allow the rose in churches because of its association with the debauchery of the declining Roman empire, but the church later changed its mind, and the rose became the symbol of martyrdom, the five petals of the wild rose representing the five wounds of Christ. St Dominic was said to have received a chaplet of roses from the Virgin Mary, and it was this chaplet that the rosary came to symbolize. The first rosaries were strings of beads made from rose petals, pressed tightly together into tiny fragrant balls.

MATERIALS

1 piece of 26-count cream linen, 10 × 8in
(25 × 20cm)
Oval frame, 8 × 6in (20 × 15cm)
Medium-weight cardboard to fit frame
Rubber-based adhesive
Felt or paper to fit frame
Adhesive or paper tape
Anchor stranded cotton – use 2 strands
throughout except for the leaf stems
and veins, which are worked in 1
strand

6ft 6in (2m) mid-green (256)

6ft 6in (2m) light green (255)

5ft (1.5m) pink (28)

5ft (1.5m) mid-pink (26)

5ft (1.5m) light pink (24)

5ft (1.5m) olive green (267)

3ft 3in (1m) fuchsia (29)

3ft 3in (1m) dark green (862)

DESIGN SIZE
6 × 4½in (15 × 11cm)

METHOD

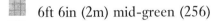

Fold the linen in half and then in half
again to find the centre. Mark the centre
of the chart and work outwards from this
point. Stitch using two strands of cotton
and working crosses over two strands of
linen both horizontally and vertically.
Follow the chart in cross stitch, but work
the leaf stems and veins in small
backstitch using one strand only.

Place the empty frame on the
cardboard and draw around the inside.
Use a craft knife to cut out the cardboard
and mount the linen on it, stretching and
folding the edges to the back of the
cardboard, where they should be glued in
place. Place the mounted picture in the
frame and cover the back with felt or
paper, which can be secured in position
with adhesive or paper tape.

*A fresh-blown musk rose; 'twas the first that
threw
Its sweets upon the summer: graceful it grew
As is the wand that Queen Titania wields.
And, as I feasted in its fragrancy,
I thought the garden-rose it far excelled;
But when, O Wells! thy roses came to me
My sense with their deliciousness was spelled;
Soft voices had they, that with tender plea
Whispered of peace, and truth and friendliness
unquelled.*
'TO A FRIEND WHO SENT ME SOME ROSES',
JOHN KEATS (1795–1821)

SUMMER FLOWERS GREETINGS CARD AND FRAMED PICTURE

This bouquet of summer flowers would work well on a dressing table set or on a sachet filled with pot pourri. Here the motif has been worked on two different counts of fabric – and I added a butterfly to the greetings card for good measure.

The decorative, culinary and therapeutic uses for flowers are virtually unlimited – you can make inks, glues, soups, bath oils, perfumes . . .

Try crystallizing rose and violet petals for decoration. All you need are the white of one egg and some caster sugar. Whisk the egg white until it is frothy and paint it on the petals with a soft paintbrush. Dip each petal in caster sugar, shake off any excess and lay the petals on a tray covered with grease-proof paper. Leave them in a warm, dry place until they are quite dry. The left-over sugar, which will be faintly perfumed, can be used in cakes in the normal way. Store the dry petals in an air-tight tin.

Forget-me-nots, lawn daisies, violets, rose petals and primroses can all be used in small quantities in salads. Try not to handle the petals too much as they bruise easily, mix them with your other salad ingredients and toss them lightly in a French dressing.

You can make your own pot pourri by drying summer flowers, chosen for their colour and fragrance, in a dust-free environment. Lay the petals in shallow trays on newspaper and turn them occasionally. On the first day keep them at a temperature of about 90°F (32°C), then at 75–80°F (24–27°C). Leave them for two or three weeks so that the petals are absolutely dry. Store in paper bags or dark jars in a cool, dry place. A little citrus fruit rind will add a delicious, fresh fragrance to your finished pot pourri.

Meadows trim with daisies pied,
Shallow brooks and rivers wide.
Towers, and battlements it sees
Bosom'd high in tufted trees,
Where perhaps some beauty lies,
The cynosure of neighbouring eyes.
L'ALLEGRO, *JOHN MILTON (1608–74)*

PRIMROSE

The commonest superstition concerning primroses is that it is unlucky to bring less than a handful at a time into the house. Among poultry breeders this is thought to endanger the young stock – either the broods will be very small or the existing birds will die. In some areas they are forbidden altogether when hens are sitting, but usually their presence is considered safe provided that there are enough of them. In Sussex it is the first bunch brought in that is important. If this contains fewer than thirteen blossoms, the hens and geese will lay only as many eggs as there are flowers. A single primrose carried indoors, or given to any person, is worst of all, for not only will this make the hens hatch only one egg out of each clutch, but it may also foretell or cause the death of a human member of the family.

The physicians of Myddfai prescribe the following remedy 'for the bite of a mad dog': 'Take primrose, pound small, express the juice under a press, and mix with milk, giving it the patient to drink nine times.' For 'a pain in a joint' they recommend: 'Take water chickweed, the leaves and blossoms of primrose, and a flintstone, pound them well together and boil with May butter; anoint the painful part with it warm. Let it be kept in an earthen pot.'

A Perfumed Basket
Place a layer of perfumed Cotton extremely thin and even on a piece of Taffety stretched in a frame; strew on it some Violet Powder, and then some Cypress Powder; cover the whole with another piece of Taffety: nothing more remains to complete the work, but to quilt it, and cut it of the size of the basket, trimming the edges with ribband.

THE TOILET OF FLORA

Small service is true service while it lasts:
Of humblest friends, bright creature! scorn not one:
The daisy, by the shadow that it casts,
Protects the lingering dewdrop from the sun.
TO A CHILD, WRITTEN IN HER ALBUM,
WILLIAM WORDSWORTH (1770–1850)

MATERIALS

Greetings card
1 piece of 26-count cream or white linen, 5 × 4in (13 × 10cm)
1 piece of light-weight cardboard
Picture
1 piece of 26-count cream or white linen, 3½ × 2in (9 × 6.5cm)
Frame
Medium-weight card to fit frame
Rubber-based adhesive
Anchor stranded cotton – use 2 strands throughout for greetings card **or** 1 strand throughout for picture, for which only half the listed quantities are required

- 20in (50cm) yellow (298)
- 20in (50cm) green (255)
- 20in (50cm) crimson (42)
- 20in (50cm) fuchsia (87)
- 20in (50cm) coral (9)
- 20in (50cm) white (1)
- 12in (30cm) blue (129)
- 12in (30cm) purple (111)
- 12in (30cm) lilac (109)
- 12in (30cm) peach (25)
- 12in (30cm) flame (10)

Butterfly
- 12in (30cm) grey (849)
- 12in (30cm) lemon (289)
- 12in (30cm) blue (118)
- 12in (30cm) camel (362)

DESIGN SIZE
Greetings card – 4 × 1¾in (10 × 4cm);
picture – 2 × 1½in (5 × 4cm);

They are the lords and owners of their faces,
Others but stewards of their excellence.
The summer's flower is to the summer sweet,
Though to itself it only live and die.
SONNETS, 94, *WILLIAM SHAKESPEARE (1564–1616)*

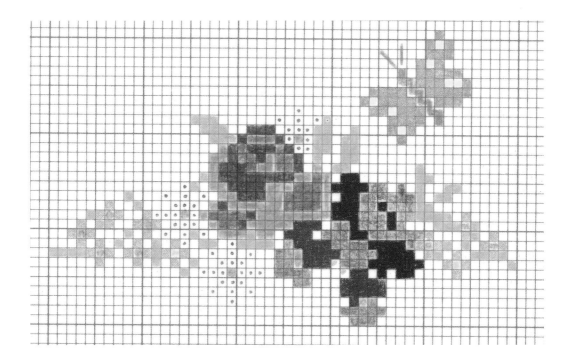

METHOD

Fold the linen in half and then in half again to find the centre. Mark the centre stitch on the chart and work outwards from this point. For the greetings card use two strands of cotton worked over two strands of linen both horizontally and vertically. For the picture use one strand of cotton worked over one strand of linen both horizontally and vertically.

MAKING UP

GREETINGS CARD

Fold the cardboard twice to make three equally sized sections. Cut an oval, 4¼ × 3¼in (10.5 × 8cm), in the centre of the middle section. Glue the finished cross stitch to the inside of the left-hand section of the cardboard and fold into position.

PICTURE

Cut a piece of cardboard to fit the frame and mount the finished cross stitch on the cardboard, turning back the edges of the linen and gluing them to the back. Secure into the frame.

By shallow rivers, to whose falls
Melodious birds sing madrigals.
and I will make thee beds of roses
And a thousand fragrant posies.
THE PASSIONATE SHEPHERD TO HIS LOVE,
CHRISTOPHER MARLOWE (1564–93)

When daisies pied and violets blue
And lady-smocks all silver-white
And cuckoo-buds of yellow hue
Do paint the meadows with delight,
The cuckoo then, on every tree,
Mocks married men; for thus sings he,
Cuckoo;
Cuckoo, cuckoo; O word of fear,
Unpleasing to a married ear!
LOVE'S LABOURS LOST, *WILLIAM SHAKESPEARE*
(1564–1616)

Who never negligently yet
Fashioned an April violet,
Nor would forgive, did June disclose
Unceremoniously the rose.
NATURE'S WAY,
SIR WILLIAM WATSON (1858–1936)

I'd be a butterfly born in a bower,
Where roses and lilies and violets meet
I'D BE A BUTTERFLY, *THOMAS HAYNES BAYLY*
(1797–1839)

SWEET PEA GUEST TOWEL

You can buy guest towels with built in Aida borders or, if you prefer, you can stitch your own border and attach it to a towel. This design would look equally pretty used vertically up the side of a photograph frame or on a pillowcase.

Sweet peas, *Lathyrus odoratus*, have, as their specific name suggests, a wonderful perfume, and their pretty, frilly heads are now grown in a vast range of colours. The sweet pea is closely related to the everlasting pea, *L. latifolius*, and narrow-leaved everlasting pea, *L. sylvestris*, but both these species are found only in pink and white forms.

The sweet pea we know today came originally from Sicily, where it was found by Father Francescus Cupani, who recorded his find in *Hortus Catholicus*, which was published in 1697. Plants were introduced into England at the beginning of the eighteenth century, but the original flowers, like their wild relatives, were of a limited range of colours and rather straggly in appearance. Silas Cole, the renowned gardener to Earl Spencer of Althorp Park in Northamptonshire, hybridized the first of the named cultivars, and in Victorian times sweet peas and mignonette were a favourite mixture for indoor decorations. The sweet pea is

said to have been the favourite flower of Danish-born Princess Alexandra, who became queen of England as the consort of Edward VII.

The sweet pea is an easy plant to grow, producing several dainty flowers on each stem and armfuls of blooms for indoors. Soak the black seeds overnight before you sow them and pinch out the tops of the plants when they are 4in (10cm) tall. They will grow in any well-drained garden soil in an open, sunny spot. For best results, sow the seeds in pots in autumn and overwinter them in cold frames for planting out the following spring.

In the language of flowers the sweet pea means 'pleasure' and 'remember me'. It is the symbol of delicacy and departure.

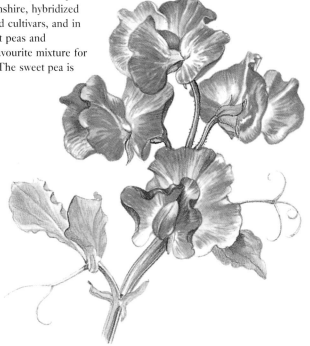

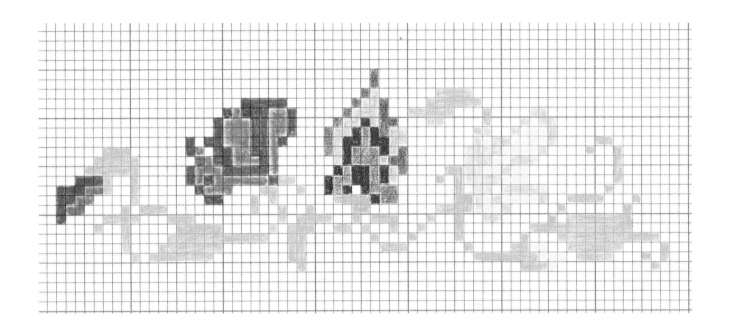

MATERIALS

1 small guest towel, approximately 10in
   (25cm) wide
1 band of 14-count Aida, 11 × 4in
   (28 × 10cm)
Anchor stranded cotton – use 3 strands
   throughout

5ft (1.5m) aqua (203)

20in (50cm) blue (118)

20in (50cm) light blue (117)

20in (50cm) mauve (110)

20in (50cm) coral (10)

20in (50cm) pink (31)

20in (50cm) gold (305)

20in (50cm) lemon (288)

METHOD

Fold the Aida in half widthways and
count down to the centre point. Mark the
centre stitch on the chart and work
outwards from this point. Stitch the
entire chart in cross stitch using three
strands of cotton. When the band is
complete, fold back the top and bottom
edges so that the band is 2¾in (7cm)
deep and fold in the short ends so that
the band fits neatly across the width of
the towel. Pin the band in position and
then stitch it neatly to the towel.

DESIGN SIZE
4¾ × 1½in (12 × 4cm)

WILD FLOWER SAMPLER

Bluebells, cornflowers and foxgloves are some of the flowers I've chosen for this simple sampler. You could, of course, use other flowers if you preferred or you could, instead of the alphabet, work a special message, using the letter chart.

BLUEBELL

Bluebells signify constancy, and this must be true, for they return year after year to carpet our woodlands and fields. There can be no better description of this flower than that given by the poet Gerard Manley Hopkins (1844–89):

> They give one a fancy of panpipes and of some wind instrument with stops – a trombone perhaps. The overhung necks – for growing they are little more than a staff with a simple crook but in water, where they stiffen, they take stronger turns, in the head like sheephooks or, when more waved throughout, like the waves riding through a whip that is being smacked – what with these overhung necks and what with the crisped ruffled bells dropping mostly on one side the gloss these have at their footstalks they have an air of the knights at chess.

Linnaeus was the first to give the bluebell the generic name *Hyacinthus*, in recognition of the association of the plant with the hyacinth of the ancient world, a flower of grief and mourning. No medical uses have been ascribed to the plant, although the juice obtained from the bulbs used to be used as bookbinders' gum, while Gerard recounts that it was used to set feathers into arrows.

COMMON NAMES: calverkeys, culverkeys, auld man's bell, ring-o'-bells, jacinth, wood bells, link.

I love the gorse and heather
And Bluebells close beside —
I'll find my cap and feather,
And kiss a Highland bride!
JOHN KEATS (1795–1821)

FOXGLOVE

The wild foxglove, *Digitalis purpurea*, is a fairy plant in folklore, and it has several other names suggesting its rather ominous character – fairy weed, dead men's bellows, bloody man's fingers and witches' thimbles. The speckles on the blossoms, like those on the cowslip and on butterfly wings, were believed to be the marks of elves' fingers. In Scotland it is considered an unlucky flower that should never be brought into a house or taken on board ship.

According to William Browne (1591–1643), Pan found a use for the flowers, when seeking gloves for his mistress:

> To keep her slender fingers from the
>   sunne,
> Pan through the pastures often times
>   hath runne
> To pluck the speckled foxgloves from
>   their stem,
> And on those fingers neatly place
>   them.

It is said to resemble an instrument of early times, the tintinnabulum, which was a ring of bells on an arched support.

Foxglove tea was an old wives' remedy for dropsy long before the plant's real medicinal value was known. Dr W. Withering, who first discovered its use in ailments of the heart, is said to have had his attention drawn to it by noticing the effects of foxglove tea prepared by Shropshire 'wisewomen'. He recorded his findings in his *Account of the Foxglove*, which was published in 1785. Doctors today, however, would probably frown on this Celtic cure for a violent headache: 'Take the leaves of foxglove, and pound with milk and mutton suet, till it becomes a plaster, apply to the head as warm as can be borne.'

COMMON NAMES: witches' gloves, dead men's bells, fairy's glove, gloves of Our Lady, bloody fingers, virgin's glove, fairy caps, folk's glove, fairy thimbles, menygellyon (elves' gloves, Wales), revebielde (foxbell, Norway), Fingerhut (thimble, Germany).

CORNFLOWER

For Russians the cornflower perpetuates the memory of a handsome young man who was beguiled by a nymph. She led him away into the golden fields of ripening corn and, jealously, turned him into a plant so that he would never charm another. The unhappy victim was named Basil or Vassili, and the Russian name for cornflower is *basilek*. Greek legend, on the other hand, relates how the child poet Cyanos, who sang of the earth and its riches, was changed by the goddess Flora into a cornflower after his death so that mankind would forever remember the poet who had so beautifully sung the praises of nature. Yet another legend states that a melancholy youth loved flowers and spent all his time making wreaths of them, dressed always in cornflower blue. He was found dead in a field, and Flora changed him into a cornflower as acknowledgement of his respect for her.

The generic name, *Centaurea*, was probably given to the plant because Chiron, the wisest of the centaurs, was said to use the plant to heal wounds.

The flower has come to be an emblem of delicacy and of the devotion of the inferior feeding upon hope, the realization of which he does not expect.

COMMON NAMES: blue knapweed, bluebottle, bachelor's button, blue bonnet, hurt sickle.

MATERIALS

1 piece of 14-count Aida, 18 × 14in
(45.5 × 36cm)
Anchor stranded cotton – use 3 strands
throughout

METHOD

Fold the Aida in half and then in half
again to find the centre. Mark the centre
point of the chart and begin to work from
this point. Stitch using three strands of
cotton throughout and working crosses
over two strands of linen both
horizontally and vertically. Follow the
chart in cross stitch, but work details on
the ladybird, caterpillar and snail in
straight stitch in brown.

Frame your work if you wish.

52ft (16m) red (335)

27ft (8.25m) green (256)

26ft 9in (8.15m) light grey (849)

18ft (5.5m) brown (352)

6ft 6in (2m) yellow (289)

5ft (1.5m) royal blue (143)

5ft (1.5m) pale pink (55)

3ft 3in (1m) blue (119)

3ft 3in (1m) pinky-mauve (85)

3ft 3in (1m) mauve (98)

3ft 3in (1m) pale blue (129)

20in (50cm) gold (304)

DESIGN SIZE
14 × 9¾in (36 × 24.5cm)

TECHNIQUES

RULES? WHAT RULES?

There are two basic rules in cross stitch. The first is that all your top stitches must slope in the same direction. The second is that all your stitches must be the same size. If you follow these two simple rules you are bound to achieve pleasing results. The rest of the information in this section will simply introduce you to the variety of materials and techniques that you can use that will transform a simple design into something special and personal and give you the means to produce a 'professionally' finished piece of work.

WORKBOX

If you are a newcomer to cross stitch fill your workbox with the following:
- ○ Evenweave fabric offcuts (see . . . *And sew on* below)
- ○ Assorted threads
- ○ Crewel needles (those with large eyes and sharp points)
- ○ Sharp scissors
- ○ Waste canvas (see . . . *And sew on* below) or transfer pencils and tracing paper
- ○ A tape measure
- ○ Cotton backing fabrics
- ○ Ribbons and laces for trimming
- ○ A rubber-based adhesive
- ○ Medium-weight cardboard
- ○ An assortment of cotton basting threads

. . . AND SEW ON

The first thing you must decide is what material you are going to sew on. This will be dictated by the size of the finished product, the intricacy of the design and the chosen yarns. I have listed here a selection of traditional background fabrics, all of which should be available in any good needlecraft shop.

CUSTOM-MADE FABRICS Several fabrics are produced especially for cross stitch. For beginners I would recommend Aida or Binca. Both these have a basket-weave construction with clearly defined holes into which you insert your needle. Aida is available in a range of different 'counts' (threads per inch), which will enable you to produce a bold, striking pattern or a delicate, intricate design. For example, if you want to work in wool and produce a boldly patterned cushion, choose 10- or 12-count Aida. A finer design worked in cotton may require 14- or 16-count Aida. Binca is available in several bright colours and has a low count to the inch, which makes it ideal for children to work with.

EVENWEAVE FABRICS Needlecraft shops stock a wide range of what are known as evenweave fabrics. 'Evenweave' simply means that there are the same number of horizontal and vertical threads in the material, making it easy to count the holes and to make your stitches the same size. Once again, you will select your fabric according to the count, which is, in this case, determined by the number of threads that you work the crosses over. For example, for fine work you would choose a fabric with a high count and work over one or two threads, while for a bold pattern you would choose a coarser fabric and decide how big you wanted your stitches to be by determining how many threads you were going to work over.

Look out for Hardanger and Linda fabrics, both of which are available in a good selection of colours and counts and are suitable for many cross stitch projects.

LINEN Linen is another evenweave fabric, although, unless it is specifically produced for needlepoint, it can be very tightly woven, and you may find it easier to work on it if you use waste canvas (see below). Counting threads on such material can turn a labour of love into a nightmare.

All linens, particularly specialist needlework linens, are very expensive, but they come in wonderful natural colours and are without equal for large projects such as table-cloths, which should, after all, become family heirlooms.

CANVAS Canvas is normally associated with needlepoint rather than cross stitch because it is coarse. Standard needlepoint canvases consist of an interlocked single thread (mono canvas) or interlocked double threads (double or Penelope canvas). You can also obtain canvases made of plastic, which can be used for three-dimensional designs, and of paper, which are for items such as Christmas decorations. It is better to work with wool rather than cotton on these canvases, and, if you do choose them for cross stitch, remember that you will have to fill in the background area of your design.

EMBROIDERY FABRIC Specialist embroidery fabrics are usually sold by the yard (metre), although you will often require only a very small piece for a project such as a greetings card. For this reason, many needlecraft shops sell bags of mixed off-cuts, which really can prove to be good value.

WHAT YOU WILL Any fabric shop will offer you a vast range of delights on which to embroider designs, but most general fabrics are 'plain weave' and are thus often impossible to 'count'. With a little experience you can safely select cottons with regular patterning such as stripes or ginghams and gauge your stitch positions according to the pattern. Do not use stretchy or knitted fabrics – your work may pucker. Once again, you must take into account the thickness and weight of your yarns before you select your material.

WASTE CANVAS

This miraculous invention will ease the way for working on a vast range of materials. It is basically very loosely woven canvas that is available in a selection of counts. The idea is that you tack (baste) it on to the background fabric of your choice so that it forms an instant grid over which you can work and so ensure that your stitches are uniformly sized. When your work is finished, you simply dampen the fabric and gently pull out the strands of canvas from under your stitches.

YARNS AND THREADS

For simplicity and because I don't think you can beat them, I have used Anchor stranded cottons for all my projects. However, there is a vast array of threads available, and your choice will add to the individuality of your work. I have listed a selection of threads and leave it to you to experiment. A major consideration is that all the threads you use are of the same thickness. If they are not, you will end up with some skimpy crosses and some fat ones, which will not be a pretty sight unless of course, you intend them to look that way.

STRANDED COTTONS All my designs use Anchor stranded cottons, which are sold in small 26ft (approximately 8m) hanks containing six individual threads. The idea is that you cut a workable length and split the threads so that you have as many strands as you need for your project. You

can, of course, mix strands of several colours together to give a subtle, shaded effect. The word floss refers to single strands of thread.

SILKS Stranded cottons are mercerized and therefore have a silky lustre. However, for the perfectionists among us, there is nothing like the real thing. Silk is available in stranded form and in twisted threads. It is expensive and not very easy to work with because the delicate fibres catch on rough skin. However, the finished effect on very fine work is quite special . . . reserve it for your masterpiece.

PEARL COTTONS Pearl cotton (coton perlé) is a single twisted, high lustre thread. There is a good selection of colours, including some with a shaded effect, and the cottons come in three different weights, which you should select according to your background fabric.

BRODER COTTON Broder cotton (coton à broder) and Danish and German flower threads are flat cottons, with a dull finish. They are smoothly spun and should not be divided. They impart a lovely 'soft' quality to your work, but they do tend to attract the dirt more quickly than mercerized cottons.

FANCIES In addition to the above, fancy threads, including lurexes, are constantly being introduced. These can be used to great effect for highlighting details, but be sure to check that the thickness of the thread will marry with the basic threads you have chosen.

GET ORGANIZED

If you are anything like me you will always pull the wrong loose end on a skein of cotton and end up with a knotted mess. To avoid this, it is a good idea to make yourself a thread organizer before beginning a project. All you need is a small strip of light-weight cardboard (an old greetings card is ideal) and a hole punch. Make a hole for each colour down the right-hand side of the card and cut your thread into manageable lengths – 20in (50cm), say. Write the colour number and, if appropriate, the symbol on the chart, next to the appropriate hole and loop your lengths of thread through it. You can then easily pull out the thread as and when you need it.

NEEDLES

For cross stitch on evenweave fabric or linen you need a selection of crewel needles. These have a sharp point and long, flat eye so that you can thread a number of strands through at a time without damaging the fabric when you push the needle through. Crewel needles are available in various sizes, and the size you use will depend on the number of threads you are intending to use. A size 24 will suit all the projects in this book.

When you work in wool on canvas you will need to use a tapestry needle. This has a blunt end and a large eye for threading. Again, you will find there are several sizes to choose from.

FRAMES

When I am working with an evenweave fabric such as Aida, I do not consider that a frame is necessary, although I do always use a frame when I am stitching on plain weave fabrics or working on a very large project.

There are various types of frame on the market, although the most popular kind for cross stitch is the hoop, which consists of two concentric circles, one of which is laid under your work and the other is laid over it and tightened with a screw to hold the fabric taut. It is a good idea to bind both rings with masking tape before you use them because the hoop may mark or distort delicate fabrics.

The second most popular type of frame consists of two parallel dowels with webbing on to which you tack the opposite ends of your fabric. The dowels are then slotted into two straight uprights, which can be tightened to hold the dowels securely. You can rotate the dowels to move the fabric up and down and to keep it taut.

SEE THE LIGHT

One miracle of modern science that I would not be without is the daylight bulb. My first needlework book (completed when I was hitting forty) resulted in an introduction to an optician, and now I sport some rather severe-looking half-moon spectacles! The problem is that most of us only have the evening available to stitch in, and good light, especially when you are counting stitches, is essential. Daylight bulbs are definitely a solution, and if you combine them with a custom-made magnifying lamp on an anglepoise-type stand, life becomes much more comfortable (see Stockist Information). You can also buy special holders for your charts and no end of other accessories to take the strain out of your work.

CHARTS

These are simple to follow. Remember that every square represents one stitch and every colour or symbol represents the colour in the key.

SIZING YOUR DESIGN

For each of the designs in this book I give the actual size of the motif that you will achieve if you work on my recommended background fabric. However, it is quite simple to re-size the motif by changing the count of the fabric you use. There is an easy way to work out the finished size according to your chosen fabric. Let's take the pansy chart as an example. First, count the number of stitches across at the widest point; on this chart it is 38 stitches. Now count the number of stitches down; it is 53. If you were going to work this design on 28-count linen over two threads, you would need to halve the count to determine the number of stitches to the inch. On 28-count linen it would be 14 stitches to the inch. You should now divide the number of stitches on your chart by the number of stitches to the inch – that is, 38 stitches divided by 14=2.71in (approximately 7cm) wide by 53 stitches divided by 14=3.78in (approximately 9.5cm) deep. When you are working on Aida you simply divide the count by the number of stitches; there is no need to halve it.

You should also remember to add at least 1in (2.5cm) of extra fabric on all sides of each project to allow for backing or, if it is a picture, for mounting.

TRANSFERRING DESIGNS

If you do not wish to work with waste canvas you can easily transfer the image with a water-erasable transfer pencil (these are available from needlework shops and haberdashers) and some tracing paper. First, test your fabric by drawing a cross on the tracing paper. Place this face down on the fabric and press it with a warm iron. If this takes to the fabric, you can then trace your complete design and transfer it. There are some wonderful coloured transfer pens and paints on the market, so you could trace or paint the design in full colour and then transfer it to the fabric by ironing (see Stockist Information).

CENTRING

Throughout the book I have suggested that you find the centre of the fabric by folding it vertically and horizontally. For absolute precision, it is a good idea to tack (baste) a line of stitches along the centre thread in both directions. Always work away from the centre unless the instructions specify otherwise.

BEGINNING YOUR WORK

You should now be almost ready to begin, but before you practise your stitching, make sure that:
- ○ Your hands are spotlessly clean
- ○ Your coffee is sitting safely on a table at least a yard (a metre) from your work
- ○ Your dog is not about to pounce on you (and your work) with muddy paws
- ○ Your cat is not sitting behind you moulting
- ○ Your clothing is not shedding filaments of fabric onto your work

STITCHING

Remember the first rule of cross stitch – that all the top stitches slope in the same direction. This can be achieved either by working a row of bottom stitches in one direction and then coming back along the row in the opposite direction or by working each complete cross individually. How you work will depend on how many stitches you have in a row before the colour changes. You can begin in any direction, but always insert your needle after the correct number of threads in your background material. The diagram shows a cross stitch being worked over two threads.

It is a good idea to thread up several needles with different colours before you begin. This will save a great deal of time.

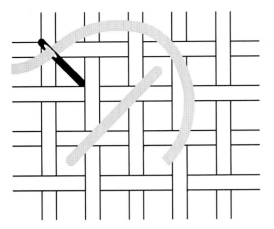

Remember that the upper stitches must all slant in the same direction.

Cross stitch is the only stitch you need to complete the majority of projects in this book. However, one or two of the designs require additional stitches. When I refer to straight stitch I mean exactly that: small, running stitches worked in a row. For backstitch you work back on yourself to achieve a continuous line. Buttonhole stitch, which is used to edge the lilac cushion, is worked by oversewing a small stitch at the edge of your fabric and slipping the needle under the previous stitch to form a horizontal line of thread along the edge between the stitches.

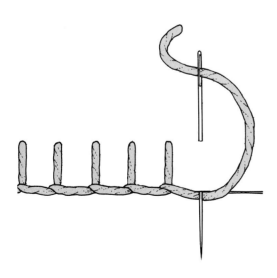

Use buttonhole stitch to create a neat, firm edge.

STRETCHING

I did not find it necessary to block any of the projects in this book. However, if you do find the shape of your work is slightly distorted, place it, face down, on a sheet of blockboard, which you should cover with a towel or sheet, and pull it into shape by inserting rustproof tacks at 1in (2.5cm) intervals. Dampen your work with a sponge or spray and leave it to dry.

Because cross stitch fabric is very soft, when you are framing projects it is usually quite simple to stretch your finished work into shape on a backing board and glue it in position with a rubber-based adhesive. Similarly, finished pieces intended for book covers and folders can be pulled into shape during the making up process.

AFTERCARE

If you have ignored all my golden rules and let the cat tiptoe across your work, you will have to wash it. **Always** check the colour fastness of the thread and fabric you have used and follow the manufacturer's instructions. Anchor threads are reputed to be fast-dyed and can be machine washed at 96°F (35°C), but you must also take the instructions for washing the background fabric into account. As a general rule, always avoid bleach and biological powders and do not tumble dry. When you iron your work, always put a towel under your work so that the stitches are not flattened and steam press, or use a damp cloth, ironing on the wrong side of the work only.

STOCKIST INFORMATION

Kits for some of the projects in this book are available by mail order. The kits contain the correct size fabric, Anchor stranded cottons and a sewing needle. For full details and prices, write to:

    Melinda Coss
    Ty'r Waun Bach
    Gwernogle
    Dyfed
    West Wales SA32 7RY (tel: 0267 202 386)

Anchor stranded cottons and Aida fabrics are available from:

    Coats Patons Crafts
    P.O. Box McMullen Road
    Darlington
    Co. Durham DL1 1YQ
or Coats & Clark Inc
    30 Patewood Drive
    Suite 351
    Greenville
    South Carolina 29615

Transfer pens, paints, needlework fabrics and lots more available from:

    Atlascraft Ltd
    Ludlow Hill Road
    Melton Road
    West Bridgford
    Nottingham NG2 6HD

A gorgeous selection of miniature frames, jars, pill boxes, paperweights and jewellery blanks are available from:

    Framecraft Miniatures Ltd
    148 High Street
    Aston
    Birmingham B6 4US
or Ireland Needlecraft Pty Ltd
    2–4 Keppel Drive
    Hallam
    Victoria 3803
    Australia
or Danish Art Needlework
    PO Box 442
    Lethbridge
    Alberta TIJ 3ZI
    Canada
or Anne Brinkley Designs Inc
    246 Walnut Street
    Newton
    Massachusetts 02160
    USA

Evenweave fabrics are available from:

    Joan Toggitt Ltd
    35 Fairfield Place
    West Caldwell
    New Jersey 07006
    USA

Greetings card blanks are available from:
  Impress
  Slough Farm
  Westhall
  Halesworth
  Suffolk IP19 8RN

Daylight bulbs and magnifying lamps are available from:
  Daylight Studios
  223a Portobello Road
  London W11 1LU

Ribbons are available from
  Ribbon Designs
  42 Lake View
  Edgware
  Middlesex

All other trimmings can be obtained from general department stores worldwide.

BIBLIOGRAPHY

I consulted the following books in the course of researching information on the flowers and their folklore, recipes and remedies.

Addison, Josephine, *The Illustrated Plant Lore*, Sidgwick & Jackson Ltd, London, 1985

Bremness, Lesley, *The World of Herbs*, Ebury Press Ltd, London, 1989

Chwast, Seymour and Blair Chewing, Emily, *The Illustrated Flower*, Omnibus Press, London, 1977

Ewart, Neil, *The Lore of Flowers*, Blandford Press, Poole, 1982

Grieve, Mrs M., *A Modern Herbal* (edited and introduced by C.F. Leyel), Jonathan Cape, London, 1931

Palaiseul, Jean, *Grandmother's Secrets: her Green Guide to Health from Plants*, Penguin Books Ltd, Harmondsworth, Middlesex, 1976

Pickles, Sheila, *The Language of Flowers*, Pavilion Books Ltd, London, 1990

Powell, Claire, *The Meaning of Flowers*, Jupiter Books, London, 1977

Pughe, John, *The Herbal Remedies of the Physicians of Myddfai*, Llanerch, 1987 (first published 1861)

Radford, E. and M.A., *The Encyclopedia of Superstitions* (edited and revised by Christina Hole), Hutchinson & Co. Ltd, London, 1961

Rohde, Eleanour Sinclair, *The Scented Garden*, The Medici Society, London, 1931

Skargan, Yvonne, *A Garland of Wild Flowers*, A. & C. Black, London, 1980

Skinner, Charles M., *Myths and Legends of Flowers, Trees, Fruits and Plants*, C.J. Lippincott, Philadelphia and London, 1913

ACKNOWLEDGEMENTS

The author would like to award gold stars to the following

For their excellent stitching – Mrs D.G. Bryant, Mrs Valerie Clark, Leanne Eden, Mrs Evans, Mrs Gibson, Mrs S. Jordan, Mrs J. Lewis, Carolyn Palmer, Mrs Anne Peterson, Jean Tanner and Mrs T. Sleap; for her lovely photography – Di Lewis; for her patient editing, stitching and research – Lydia Darbyshire; for her beautiful illustrations – Rosanne Sanders; for their generous samples – Coats Patons Crafts, Framecraft, Impress and Daylight Studios; for her advice and friendship – Eve Harlow. And a big round of applause for the team at Anaya and my friend and assistant Pat Groves, who's seen me through – despite my constant nagging.

INDEX

Page references in *italics* denote illustrations.